Autumn
Corridors

Larry G. Straub

BridgewayBooks

AUTUMN CORRIDORS
PUBLISHED BY BRIDGEWAY BOOKS
2100 KRAMER LANE, SUITE 300
AUSTIN, TEXAS 78758

For more information about our books, please write to us, call
512.478.2028, or visit our website at www.bookpros.com.

Library of Congress Control Number: 2006933197

ISBN-13: 978-1-933538-68-6
ISBN-10: 1-933538-68-6

TABLE OF CONTENTS

ACKNOWLEDGMENTS

I would first and foremost like to acknowledge my family, both my traditional and step families. Without their love and support I would not have been the man to write this story and would not in fact have had this beautiful story to write at all.

I would also like to thank the Schartz family, in particular my cousins and uncles. It was when I watched as they read excerpts of this story for the first time that I knew I was onto something really special. A special thanks to Gary Schartz for being the first Schartz family member to read the preliminary draft. His initial enthusiasm for this project helped inspire me from that point.

A special thank you to my editorial team Therese Davis, Hillary Straub, Linda Hart, Jeffrey Hart, and Jeff Meister. Very special thanks to Paul Hedlund for the incredible insights that helped me take this project to the next level.

And finally, thank you to my wife of twenty years, Julie. Without her love and support for my dream, this book would not have been possible.

Foreword

This book is not a commercial project; I have no delusions of being a best-selling author. I write this story to solidify concepts, ideas, and theories which I think are important and will hopefully serve others well at crucial points in their life. I write this book with the hope that it might give someone insight into why we live and why we inevitably die, and why doing each well (living and dying) is vitally important. I write this book ultimately and with humility to offer at least a guess at God's design.

Additionally, I write this story because it is important. It probably will not prove to be important on the world stage or even nationally. However, it will hopefully be important to my family as well as the Schartzes. Our family histories are tied tightly by blood as well as tradition; hopefully, this book will help further that bond.

THE LETTER

Finally, I write this story because of a correspondence I received, one that literally changed my life. This letter came from a former student who did not wish her identity known. (I don't even know which university I was teaching at when our paths crossed, and I have not and will not pursue attempting to find out).

Dear Professor Straub,

It is with a sadness and humility that I write this letter to you. You see, I was a student of yours in the past couple of years.

I was a student who was blessed to be in your class when you told the incredible story of your uncle's death and the impact it had on your life.

You may have noticed me because I am sure I stood out in the classroom that night. I would have been the only one in class with dry eyes and whose bottom lip was not quivering. I was the only student in class who sat there emotionless, listening to what I thought of at the time as a highly inappropriate story to be telling in an educational setting. I may have even commented on it on the evaluation that I filled out for the class, although I am not entirely sure. However, it is this last statement that bothers me the most and is the reason I feel it necessary to write to you.

The fact is, I am not that arrogant girl that sat in your class that night; I am a much more humble, more mature person than I was that night not so long ago. What is the big change you might wonder? The difference is that my father was diagnosed with terminal cancer less than three months following the conclusion of that class and six months after that he was gone.

As I went through that experience, I felt numb and totally lost, until one night while setting by his bedside, I remembered that remarkable story you told in class. I not only remembered it; I began to reflect on it, the fact that a death can hold many wonderful lessons if one is only open to them. That if a person can keep their perspective through it all, it could end up resulting in some very positive even life changing experiences.

As I reflected on those lessons you attempted to teach that night, I also began to watch and take notice. I crawled out from under my grief and onto a perch high above it all and began to watch amazing events take place. A sister that became closer to my father than she had ever been. Family sharing stories and histories, while other family members found resolution concerning long running disputes. Finally, making sure that I treasured the time I had remaining with my father, making sure that nothing was left unsaid. You were totally correct when you said, in death many times "we finish falling in love".

I just wanted to thank you for taking the chance to share that very personal part of your life with our class. It was evident that it is very difficult for you, and it takes a lot out of you. And by all means do not let an arrogant; know it all like me keep you from sharing that story with all the people you can muster the courage to share it with.

Thank you and God bless you and your family.

———

After receiving this letter, I was inspired to move ahead with this project. If this little story could have that kind of impact on one person (especially a skeptic), maybe it could impact others as well. Periodically, I tell the core of the story in classes I teach—not many, mind you, because it takes a lot out of me and I grapple with the appropriateness of it. When I have mustered the fortitude to tell it, the depth of emotion that it inspires in the students present has always overwhelmed me.

THE STORY

This story has as its basis the deaths of two people that were very close to me, my mother and (her brother) my uncle. However, even though this is the base of the story, it is not in reality the story itself, just as the crucifixion of Christ wasn't the main focus of the life of Jesus. The crucifixion was just the vehicle to an end, it was the resurrection that was the real story. Thousands upon thousands of men had died in that gruesome, tortuous manner, only one had risen after death.

This is not a story about death, it is a story about the ultimate answers concerning life and its relation to death. These answers came to me by way of these two unrelated but remarkable events.

The Corridors of Life

Winds through the corridors blow.
Winds of change, winds of controversy, winds of
    happiness, hope, and despair.
Winds of love and of hate.
The corridors we walk, the many corridors of Life.

The **Springtime** of our lives brings corridors of
    grade schools, middle schools, and our child-
    hood homes.
Corridors filled with innocence, wonderment,
    magic, growth, and excitement.

The **Summer** of our life brings the corridors of
    colleges, dormitories or apartment buildings,
    corporate offices, law firms or manufacturing
    plants, honeymoon and birthing suites, and
    hopefully our first homes.
The corridors of power and influence, pride,
    and arrogance...doors flown wide open at
    our approach.
Corridors that will lead us to believe that all
    things are possible.

Autumn corridors fill our lives with dream homes;
    vacation homes, management, partnerships,
    factory floors, hospitals, and the many failed
    and fulfilled dreams.
These corridors often times lead to disillusion-
    ment and a readjusting of our priorities.
Corridors that introduce us to the reality that
    there is no magic, that we are impotent and

powerless in the face of death, destiny, and the many other forces that impact our lives.

Winter…winter brings us to the last corridors we will walk. The corridors of nursing homes, funeral homes, retirement communities, grandchildren, and our children's first homes.

These corridors will lead to humility, faith, understanding, maturity, and a renewed sense of wonder at the world and finally a deepening of our emotions and faith that can only come with a scarcity of time.

Yes we will walk them all, the intriguing and treacherous corridors of life. And if we are lucky, we will not walk alone.

We will walk with parents, children, grandchildren, neighbors, friends, and teachers. And hopefully and through it all, we will walk with the Prince of Peace, the Great I Am.

Prologue

I walked into his hospital room on a Sunday afternoon. There he lay, my uncle Junior, on a hospital bed alone in his room. His eyes were closed; he was in a light sleep and had not noticed my presence. My first reaction was that of a scared child, to quietly back out of the room, which I in fact did. I thought for a moment or two about what to do next.

He was one of my closest uncles, he was lying in the room next to me dying of cancer, and I was to be alone with him for the first time. I had seen him in the hospital on other occasions over the past week, but those times there were always other people present. Aunts, cousins, brothers, sisters, friends, we talked about special times together; many times Junior just listened with a gleam in his eye as if to acknowledge the replay of key events in everyone's shared experience. Sometimes he would talk, though he was in a weakened state.

But this Sunday visit was to be the first time I would be alone with him; what do you say to a person who probably has less than a week to live? I was absolutely terrified at the prospect of facing this challenge.

After all, this was in reality the first death I had had to face. I was not being shielded from the reality of it as I had been many years earlier at the passing of my mother. This time I had to be part of it and I knew that. This was one of those rights of passage we all must face no matter how much we dread it, watching our first person die. To finally come to terms with our own mortality, to get a keen sense of our impotence in the face of our own lives and ultimately our deaths. I knew I needed to face this challenge but being alone with my uncle was just too much. Not me, not now. This life lesson would have to wait.

"Go to him…"

I backed quietly away from the door and slowly walked down the hall, feeling like a complete coward. I was approaching the exit door when I caught the eye of the nurse working the front reception desk of the hospital. She knew who I was from past visits; I could tell she knew the turmoil going through me at that moment. She gave me a compassionate glance, a look that said "it's all right. I know what you are going through and I won't think less of you if you walk out that door." After all she knew he was in there alone; he was one of only a handful of patients in the hospital that particular day.

"…time to let it go…"

She had let me off the hook; she had made it acceptable for me to go through that door and not come back until it was safe and comfortable again. But with that look came the reality that I needed to go back, to face my fear and spend time with my Uncle Junior. As much as I needed to leave, what he needed, he needed more. He needed love, compassion, and companionship to help fill the time he had left.

"Is that what she said?…"

Upon this realization I turned and walked back down the hall, one that now seemed much longer than it actually was. I didn't look at the nurse again, partly out of determination to do what was needed, partly out of the shame of being caught in a weak moment.

As I walked back toward my uncle's room, I walked back into a moment in time...one that would change my life forever. It was a rather un-dramatic moment in a way; however, a phrase, a few choice words that would put into perspective the fundamentals of life...and of death.

Over the course of one amazing week, a mother (long gone) and a brother (on the brink of death), would reach across the void between the living and the dead to teach a final lesson to a son and a nephew. This week would bring those two deaths nearly twenty years apart, together in time and would award to me a definition and perspective that had not existed in my life to that point.

Join me as through this amazing story I take you full force down the corridors...the corridors of life.

Part One

Spring Corridors—Life as It Was...

The Springtime of our lives brings corridors of
    grade schools, middle schools, and our child-
    hood homes.
Corridors filled with innocence, wonderment,
    magic, growth, and excitement.

Chapter 1

The Family & Towns

At times it seemed as if it was only a dream. My boyhood...a distant past filled with carefree days, days spent playing with friends and worrying about those all-important things that occupy a young boy's mind.

Those days were gone now.

What lay ahead now was the hard work of living after the death of a loved one. That time soon after...when each breath feels like a chore, when you find no joy in all the things that once brought you joy, when the only thoughts that fill your mind are about how to move beyond the intense pain that now fills every fiber of your existence.

———

It is probably fitting before we begin, that I introduce you to some key players in this true-life melodrama. First, I will introduce myself and then my family. This section of the book will be intentionally brief—we are not the focus of this story, we are merely unwitting players caught up in these dramatic events. But I do feel it is important to know something about us so that key events will fit better at later stages in the book.

THE AUTHOR

I am happily married to my wife Julie and have two wonderful children, Hillary and Brantley. I am in my mid forties
and my daughter is fifteen, my son eleven. My wife and I have
always had a very balanced and loving relationship and are so
alike that at times it is unnerving. We maintain a very comfortable lifestyle in Salina, Kansas, a town of about 50,000 people
located an hour from Great Bend and a little over two hours
west of Kansas City. A nice sized, small city, Salina has the relative good fortune of having two major Interstate highway systems intersect at its doorstep.

As for myself, the author, I am a full time businessman and
part time professor of business working in an adjunct capacity
for two universities in Kansas. My business is a company called
Straub International, Inc., a multi-store agricultural equipment
company with approximately 35 million dollars in sales out of
our six locations in Kansas. It is a fourth-generation family business in which I, my father, brother, and sister-in-law all work, in
addition to a small number of other partners in the business. I
am the Chairman and Chief Executive Officer of the company;
we have over one hundred employees and have been in business for sixty-one years.

I fancy myself to be a somewhat well rounded individual. I
am a former collegiate tennis player and still play competitively,
and was a somewhat accomplished musician in my earlier years.
I am an academic with an MBA and Master of Science from two
different universities; these degrees afford me the privilege of
teaching at the university level.

This being said, in relation to the big picture I do not consider
myself an exceptional person by any means. I am a little better
than some and a little worse than others—by most measures, a
fairly average individual.

THE STRAUBS

While it may sound a bit cliché, I have to say that my family
is my rock, not only my wife and kids, but also my brothers, sis-

ters, dad, step mom, and stepsisters. I was blessed not only with a wonderful mother who was taken from me too early, but then the Lord also blessed me with a step family that was able to take the "work in progress" of my life and help complete it.

My Father

My dad was unable to finish high school due to the demands of his family's central Kansas farming operation; however, he is blessed with a truly remarkable, natural intellect for business. I had to earn two graduate level degrees to finally feel I could communicate on a level equal to his. My father has always possessed this very impressive intelligence; nevertheless it could never be on a par with his heart. He is a man who knows no strangers and will always try to help someone in need.

Whatever my father gave up in formal education he more than compensated for in his willingness and ability to work hard and to learn. He always held out the goal of owning his own company, and he knew he had to work hard and pay his dues to make that happen. He worked many hours with his employer and always seemed to have some small business venture going on the side; these provided the family with added income as well as giving him an opportunity to refine his developing business skills.

We struggled many times as a family while I was growing up, but deep down I think my father loved the challenge of it all. He always had the confidence (bordering on quiet arrogance) that no matter what came our way, he was smart and hard working enough to find a way through it.

My father has stayed true to his blue collar roots throughout his life, even after achieving a significant level of success in his life. He has always possessed a stubborn pride and sense of obligation, doing whatever it took to keep us fed and sheltered, and he took care of the many extras that would not have otherwise been affordable. My father told me many times through the years that he probably enjoyed the challenging times of his life the best, when we had to pull together as a family and hold on tight until we got through the rough waters. He insisted then, and I agree now, that we would one day look back on those as some of the best days of our lives.

My Mother

My mother, Barbara Jane Schartz, as one of the two key players in the story, will be detailed a bit more than the others at this juncture.

My mother was the oldest of six children born to two colorful and hard-living parents. By hard-living I mean they lived life fast, drinking a bit more than they should and partying a little harder than most. The Schartz family at one time had quite a bit of money, by way of my great grandfather, but as with many families it slowly dissipated as the generations passed.

As I look back, my early childhood did not seem that unusual to me. Everyone seemed nice enough (definitely a merry bunch) but there was certainly a darker side; alcohol was the undertow of it all. I do not mean to portray it as totally out of control, but it was probably close at times.

Mom, I believe, was at times the default caretaker for her brothers, almost a surrogate mother. I think she took it as her job to keep life normal for her younger brothers, to shield them and herself from as much as possible; a close bonding relationship formed between them as a result. My grandparents, regrettably, passed away early in my life, well before I was able to define a relationship with either of them.

My mother always suffered from a nervous condition that later in life contributed to many health problems. She never battled alcoholism, primarily because my father helped guide her away from that life; his family too had major problems with that disease and he would have no part of it.

As I think back on my relationship with my mother, it is in some ways faceless. By that I mean it is a bit of a blur, likely because it didn't have a chance to fully develop. Due to her nervous condition and myriad health problems, I think it was very difficult for her to raise younger children in particular. And I believe that my and my siblings' relationships with our mother would have gotten better as we grew older and would have continued to improve as we became adults.

Over thirty years after her death, in a conversation with my father, he explained to me the love and sense of loss he still feels, even after all these years. He recounted stories of the night they met and shared a poem he had recently composed expressing the depth of his feelings. Even though he has been very happily married for the past twenty-five years to an extraordinary woman, my stepmother, it cannot totally fill the void left when my mother passed on. She must have been an incredibly special woman to have so captivated his heart and soul.

The Rest of the Clan

The last members of my family (other than my step family which will be introduced at a later point in the book) are my older siblings Linda and Ron. My sister Linda is the oldest, six years my senior; we have always gotten along well and have been very close, however it is fair to say we have grown even closer as adults. My brother and I were closer growing up, primarily due to what we had in common—a love of games, sports, and an all-around good sibling bond. Through our day-to-day business relationship via our company, we have remained extremely close through the years.

My nieces and nephews are all very special to me. I have six in total and we have all maintained a special bond throughout our lives. My wife and I, and eventually our kids, used to throw what we referred to as "kids night" parties for all of our nieces and nephews. We had all the kids over at night to watch movies, play games, make home movies, spoof commercials, and anything else we could think of. These were very special times. Eventually as they entered their teen years, they began to grow away from such events; however, the nights and times we had with them in their younger years remain treasured memories for all of us.

THE SCHARTZES

The Schartz families who will play prominently in this story are uncles, aunts, and first cousins. There was Uncle Junior, my mom's brother, and his wife Pat. Junior was a wonderful man with a keen sense of humor and a zest for life. My cousins, five of them—two boys and three girls—were as close as you could get growing up. My mother had four other brothers, Clayton (the oldest brother), Allen (the youngest), Dennis, and Max (who is now deceased).

My cousins and my family remain close to this day, although the demands of our lives and families have made it tough to stay as close as we once were (as kids). All five of Junior's kids have two things in common. One is a love of their hometown, where all still live to this day. The other is their father's great sense of humor and a robust laugh to match.

THE TWO TOWNS

The towns of Great Bend and Ellinwood are the primary Kansas cities in which this life's drama plays out; they are inseparably linked both in terms of my life story and their economic and community fortunes.

THE KANSAN

Before we get to the towns, let me preface by talking about the state. The two towns in a way are a reflection of the state in which they are located; therefore, it would be relevant to discuss a typical Kansan.

What I respect most about Kansans is the fact that they are not overly impressed with anyone, least of all themselves. Periodically, a lost celebrity will find his/her way to the state; Kansans will watch with some amusement as he blows into our world and back out as quickly as the airlines or the speed limits will allow. Kansans are polite and respectful; however, they usually tire quickly of the invasion and are anxious to get back to their own world, a world without the whirl of celebrity, power lunches, and extreme pressures of urban life.

Kansas is a state of vivid contrasts. The northeast has one of the most affluent metropolitan areas (Johnson County/Kansas City) in the United States. There are other pockets of prosperity, surprisingly affluent and even beautiful areas of the state in countless university and college towns.

Unfortunately they are the exception. What defines Kansas

in most people's minds is the rather flat, treeless landscape in the western half of the state. In fact, a recent study by scientists from a university in Texas seems to have proven that Kansas is scientifically proven to be as flat as a pancake (actually flatter). Even a former Governor joined the bandwagon recently, endorsing a plan put forth by a couple of East Coast scholars called "The Buffalo Commons" which proposes that much of the western half of the state should be returned to the buffalo (needless to say the plan was not received enthusiastically by the fine folks in Western Kansas).

Surprisingly, Kansans take this all rather well. Kansans have a stubborn independence, a self-contained assurance that gives them a calm sense of confidence. They know they have a very good thing—more space than anyone else, open roads to drive (the type of winding roads seen in roadster commercials, not the gridlocked traffic that is most city dwellers' reality), and more importantly no one knows (or cares) what we have.

And that is just fine with most Kansans. Yes, they want some growth, but they can do without the runaway growth that has changed some formerly rural areas to almost unrecognizable levels. Most Kansans feel that when the world gets too nuts, and it surely will, then we will have to fight to keep our soul and our borders intact.

As I talk of the two towns and some of the places of my childhood and early adulthood, notice that the DNA flows through from the state to the counties, the towns, and the people. The pride, stubbornness, and independence are the same as that possessed by the original homesteaders who pioneered and settled such an inhospitable landscape in the first place.

"The Bend"

Great Bend is a small college town of 15,500 souls and is the county seat of Barton County. It is a typical small town in many ways, the problems, charms, and quality of life as many others. It is named, as are so many towns in this part of the country, by way of an interesting geographic feature, the Arkansas River. Great Bend is located at the northern most point of the Arkansas River, it V's dramatically north as if to catch this one last town before it dives south through Wichita and out of the state toward Oklahoma. That is why some in the town refer to Great Bend as "the Bend" and life time citizens as "Benders."

It has a laid back style that can be easily romanticized and a city layout both somewhat rough at its worst, yet with the feel of a charming Midwestern city at its best. The town was founded on agriculture and ranching, as were many of the towns in Kansas, and its fortunes took a turn for the better when oil was discovered in the early to mid 1900s.

Most of my life in Great Bend took place on Broadway Boulevard; that is where my kids were born (at the hospital), where I owned two houses in early adulthood, and quite possibly where I will be buried someday (at the cemetery). Broadway Boulevard is the street where life meets in the Bend. It runs west to east for the length of the city, a stately boulevard separated by grass-covered medians strategically planted with Red Bud trees, and it runs through the primary residential area. It is a beautiful drive in the spring, when the trees are in full bloom.

The original moneyed class of Great Bend lived along Broadway Boulevard, the doctors, bankers, lawyers, and successful businessmen. This street is a throwback to a "Rockwellian" lifestyle of large open lawns, tree lined streets and big, welcoming porches. On a hospitable spring, summer, or fall evening it feels the way neighborhood streets must have been like in another era; families and couples walking aimlessly, people stopping by for a chat with a neighbor or acquaintance, the smell of fresh cut grass.

The Square

Broadway hits its culmination when it intersects with Main Street and happens by the square, the 1800s era city center. This is both a traditional town center and courthouse square, simply packed with charm. It is very well kept and has been extensively "street scaped" with turn-of-the-century style streetlights. With its band shell and amphitheatre seating area, a huge water fountain in the plaza, and a couple of civil-war-era statues, it is indeed the center of life in this town.

As in any small town, legends persist, some even comical.

One such legend has the statue of "Reb" (a statue of a nameless civil war soldier) coming down from his perch in the square once a year around Christmas and having a drink at the pool hall a block from the square. The pool hall is now a dining establishment and though the legend hasn't been updated accordingly, they do serve beer. Hopefully, "Reb" is not too particular (it should be duly noted that there have been no confirmed sightings of this phenomenon).

The downtown business center unfortunately has seen better days, specifically when oil money flowed as freely as the oil itself. Great Bend in the tradition of other oil cities in Texas and Oklahoma has seen tough times in the past two decades. However, the town has a resiliency that is not only admirable, I would call it amazing. Nothing comes easy economically for a town that missed the Interstates, somewhat like the towns in the 1800s that missed the railroads. Towns like Great Bend have to literally scrap for everything that comes their way, but they do it and do not complain. They possess a pioneer spirit that they come by honestly and hold onto with vigilance.

Charlie's Place

Much to my wife's chagrin, one of the places I found compelling and entertaining in my thirties (and to this day when I visit) was a watering hole by the name of Charlie's Place. This is a joint (in the classical sense), a bar you could easily adopt as part of your social regimen, and a place where people come to celebrate their week's successes or salve their wounds of defeat. Charlie's is a place that has the look of…well, of a pub, a bar, a watering hole, inside and out.

It is located in a turn-of-the-century-era building just a stone's throw from the courthouse square, and named after a rather undistinguished barrister by the name of Charlie Carol. His most distinguished feature was the hat he wore, present in all the old pictures. In fact, it seemed as much a part of his head as the hair attached to his scalp. I am not sure whether Charlie actually enjoyed libations, but by the luck of the draw and the fact that the building is located in his former office space, he now has a monument to his memory that caters to those in need of a drink. His pictures grace the walls of the bar and his old law books are placed impressively on book shelves at the back of the bar by the pool tables (never have I noticed an impaired and disheveled patron perusing their pages, but I am always on the lookout).

The bar itself has a somewhat distinguished air in its interior with 20 foot high sculpted ceilings, brick floors, and a carved wood bar running impressively along the entire south wall. It is the center of the town's social life, such as it is. When I return to the Bend, I go there to catch up, to see what's new and happening.

Despite its rather staid surroundings, it still has many of the appointments of a traditional bar—the TVs, pool table, dart boards and even a female mannequin with a wig of flowing red hair, adorned with a bra and lacy panties. The general rule among the patrons: when you had had enough to drink to start making eyes at her, it was time to call it a night.

The proprietor of this wondrous establishment is a rather distinguished looking gentleman by the name of Tim Miller. To Mr. Miller the bar is a part-time venture, as much a community service and labor of love as a profitable business. Tim is an oilman and cattleman who raises Texas Longhorns. He has a chameleon-like appearance that blends as well with bankers and businessmen as with ranch hands and rough necks, and his white hair, beard, and mustache—along with his impeccable wardrobe—give him an understated charisma that people young and old are drawn to. He is a man's man who still knows how to open doors for ladies and even in this day and age (of women's liberation) could call a woman "darlin'" and have her blushing like a school girl. Overall, his swagger, confidence, and toughness are reminiscent of characters portrayed by John Wayne.

Walking down the hall toward my uncle's room,
I happened to feel a breeze from an open window,
at that moment my gaze was drawn to the window
and what lay beyond.

Outside in the distance I could hear locusts...I grew up listening to those locusts on early evenings; it was as if they were signaling the official end to afternoon and the beginning of a lazy summer evening.

As I looked out on the front lawn of the hospital and beyond, not only did the hallway seem longer but time seemed to almost suspend. I looked beyond the lawn out onto the main street of the city of Ellinwood, a main street in the full bloom of spring.

A street that had been magical to me growing up, a street that in better, more distant times had been the scene for many festival shared by the Schartzes and the Straubs...

ELLINWOOD

The town of Ellinwood, which was and is to this day the Schartz side of my family's hometown, has approximately 2,500 people. Ellinwood is what Benders refer to as a bedroom community, but don't let the good people of Ellinwood here you say that. They have a fierce independence and believe they would be just as well off if Great Bend weren't just ten miles to the west (even though that is clearly not the case). It has been said that for a community to survive and prosper, it has to have a keen sense of pride; Ellinwood takes this a bit further. It has an un-apologetic arrogance, and I point this out with a grudging admiration. It is not rude or brash, simply self-assured—an assumed self-reliance and the belief that no matter what happens, they will be all right.

This hamlet was started as a German settlement and is over 120 years old. The Schartzes are one of the oldest family lineages in the town and region. The town is most notable for its distinctive downtown, its beautiful tree lined streets, and its stately homes and churches. It also has a wonderful richly wooded nine hole golf course that by some odd stroke of fate is cut in half by the highway. (To my knowledge no one has been killed crossing the highway while golfing, though it has claimed dogs and other small animals.) The town always reminded me of what Grover's Corner, New Hampshire—made famous in Thornton Wilder's play *Our Town*—must have felt like to grow up in.

Also present in the town of Ellinwood is the community hospital located on Main Street where Junior Schartz would pass his last days on earth.

Even though Great Bend was my boyhood home and actual hometown, Ellinwood held much mystery, adventure, and delightful memories for me. My cousins and I would literally go from one end of the town to the other on a good day, finding many things along the way to keep our young minds engaged.

Some of my fondest memories involve the yearly After Harvest Festival, the four-day festival that occurred every year after wheat harvest. It involved all the trappings of a traditional small town celebration, the parades, carnivals, cookouts, and ice cream socials. Additionally, private gatherings, and family and class reunions are conveniently scheduled in conjunction with each year's festival.

The nights spent with my cousins before the festival were especially exciting. We walked the streets at night listening to the sounds of the festival coming together. We smelled the chickens and steaks being cooked on the open grills while walking to Main Street where we watched the carnival workers put the Ferris wheel and other rides together along the streets of the downtown area. Additionally, we watched the volunteers putting up the tables for the following night's ice cream social in the band shell park along Main Street, across from the turn-of-the-century Catholic church. If we got too close, we got drafted to lend a hand, which we gladly did...anything to be part of the festive atmosphere.

The memories are so strong it seems as though it all happened just a short while ago. These were the days in which my bonds were tied forever with the Schartz clan; bonds forged on the tree-lined parks, streets, and fishing holes of this very special place. If I think long enough, I can feel the breeze and smell the fragrance of summer...in Ellinwood...with the Schartzes.

Sometimes it seemed as though we could actually feel the ghosts of previous generations brush by us as we walked down the street. Not a scary sensation at all, it was peaceful...even playful, as if we heard them apologize for the interruption as they moved by. One could easily imagine that if we get to choose where to spend eternity, this is a place one might consider.

Yet, as memorable and eventful as those times were, more unforgettable ones were yet to come with this family whose lives were so irrevocably linked to ours.

Chapter 2

Christmas with the Schartzes

Some of my fondest childhood memories involve holiday gatherings with the Schartz family, particularly Christmas celebrations. What was really amazing about the special Christmases we had growing up was that we had them at all. Most years we had lots of presents, a Christmas tree, and big celebrations. This could not have been an easy task for my father or Junior at times. We had no idea then how challenging it must have been to pull this off, but somehow they made them happen. The Christmases of my youth brought lots of food, laughter, and very special times. They were magic, and still they make me look back on my childhood with a sense of wonder.

Christmas Eve was actually the climactic day for our celebration, building to a crescendo of excitement and culminating with the opening of presents that night. All day and early evening were magical; they made us believe everything good about humanity—people were basically good and, given the desire, we could make anything happen if we wished. We felt that everyone on the planet must be sharing in our feelings of love and good will at that particular moment.

When I was about five or six years old, I received a call from Santa Claus. I remember it vividly—bells and hammering in the background, and elves arguing about toy designs and delivery schedules. It was a wonderful call; I went to bed that night and dreamed of the workings of the North Pole and the toys being built just for me.

I also recollect nights of lying on the floor listening to holiday music in the family room and just admiring the Christmas tree. Our family had one of those tinsel Christmas trees lightly flocked with a white substance that was supposed to resemble snow. We also had one of those decorative lights with the round panels in front of a light bulb, moving slowly between its three different colors. The panel would go round and round and with the lights turned low, would make the tree and room look magical. Additionally, we had a fake fireplace that my mother designed out of an old steam iron; she covered it with brick poster board and put fake fire and logs where real ones would normally have been. Even though it was artificial, I loved it. And the tree always had many gifts under it—from Thanksgiving, the stack grew continually as it got closer to Christmas Eve.

As noted earlier, what makes these events so special in hindsight is knowing now what it likely took from these special men and their wives to make these holiday gatherings happen (I think I appreciated that even at an early age). We were definitely a Christmas family; my mother, father, siblings—as well as the Schartzes—all got absolutely giddy as the month progressed and the holiday drew near. While I believed in Santa, the elves, and the reindeer, I knew where the presents (at least the majority of them) came from. My parents and what they did to provide them was no secret; they worked very hard to make these special holidays happen.

THE L.B. PRICE ROUTE

I remember, for instance, my dad working a route for the L.B. Price Company, a direct marketing company which sold many types of products direct to the consumer. This meant my father developed a route of customers in Great Bend that he saw weekly or monthly, selling, delivering, and then collecting money. I remember driving on Saturdays and Sundays with my dad as he made his calls. This was at the same time that he was working 60 to 70 hours a week as a mechanic for a truck dealership.

Many of my fondest recollections involve traveling with him on his route to sell and collect for merchandise. Many of his clients were not particularly well off; however, my dad talked about them as if they were the most important people on earth. He always possessed an inherent respect for people no matter what their circumstances, and he took great pride in helping them get things they could not normally have afforded. I proudly carry that same philosophy with me to this day. He constantly told me that it takes all different types of people to make this world work; learn to respect, appreciate, and work with as many as you can.

As a man who enjoyed meeting people and helping serve their needs, my father never complained about the added work-load and actually seemed to enjoy the experience. It has been said that he never met a stranger, and I think that was especially true in those days and still holds true. The skills he developed during this period of his life helped to lay the foundations for the successful business career that would follow.

THE MEDICINE

Another lesson I learned came by way of a grocery shop-ping excursion with my mother, one in which we had a slight mishap. My mom had many health problems during my early years; seemingly one problem after another. Many times they were serious and though never life threatening, some did in-volve surgeries. Many of these procedures required medicines and prescription drugs that at times could be rather costly.

On this particular day, while helping my mom unload gro-ceries, a bottle of medicine was dropped. I don't remember what it was or who did it; all I remember was my mom melting to the ground and crying because of what the expense would be to replace the drugs. I remember her questioning through the tears where the money would come from and how we would afford groceries the next week.

I am sure that my dad likely arrived home that night and laughed off the dilemma, calming my mom down immedi-ately. No matter how big the challenge, he always had a way of making it seem manageable; he has that skill to this day. However, at six years of age I remember going to sleep that night wondering if we would have anything to eat the next week. I remember the very real fear of that moment and I don't think I will ever forget it. To this day I am glad I had that experience; it makes me more empathetic and generous, and more understanding of people with less fortunate circumstances.

I have never forgotten those experiences and the lessons I gained from each. That is in large part why I teach; it is my L.B. Price, my way to provide some of the extras in life that might normally be out of reach for me and my family. It is my safety net should my family ever experience tough times. In this way I can help assure food on the table should the world crumble out from underneath us temporarily.

Chapter 3

Death and the Struggle for Survival

As I continued toward the room I felt myself melt back in time to another day, another death, another corridor, that corridor left unexplored.

The vivid imagery of that day so long ago...transcended the present time. I was thirteen again...I could hear the gravel under my feet, feel the breeze on my face, it was as if I could even smell the tar under the gravel.

And finally, sadly, I could hear the voice of the priest, as clearly as I had when he was standing just a few feet in front of me...

When I became conscious of my physical presence again, I felt as though I hadn't been able to take a breath for minutes. It was as if someone had sucker punched me in the chest with a fist or heavy object, one that came out of nowhere and made it that much worse to recover from. As I began to breathe again, I smelled the hospital again, the strong smell of antiseptics and sterilizers; this was odd in that I was in the open air on the roof of Wesley Medical Center in Wichita, Kansas.

For some reason it did not strike me as odd when the priest who had visited us periodically over the past few days had asked me if I had wanted to see the roof of the hospital. It seemed somewhat adventurous and a welcome break from the tedious routine that had occupied our days since arriving at the hospital. Being from a small town and a thirteen-year-old boy, I was somewhat excited to see the city from a different vantage point. After all, in Great Bend there's no opportunity to look down from the top of a tall structure such as this multi-story building. The priest and I had become somewhat close in the past couple of days—as close as you can become to any person within a short period of time.

No, it did not strike me as odd at the time which is probably why I didn't notice the foreboding glance my father gave us as we left the waiting room area. However, as I replayed the day's events in my mind later, I remembered that brief look. Knowing finally what it foretold, I felt somewhat embarrassed that I was so clueless. It's the way a person must feel when he or she loses his job and, in replaying the events of the fateful day—the nervous chatter with coworkers, the lack of eye contact—finally realizes he was the only one that did not know what was coming.

In retrospect it seems obvious now that my father, the priest, and my family had attempted to prepare me for this outcome (the death of my mother), probably even telling me what the outcome would be. I was likely in denial or not clearly comprehending the message they were attempting to impart. The priest's job now was to make sure I knew the situation and grasped it fully. This time...in that respect, he was successful... he had hit the mark.

And with that...I was unprepared for the reality. I was trying to keep my emotions to myself and stay calm; the fact that I could not breathe regularly betrayed me almost immediately.

"Damn it Jim!" ... (what?)

I knew my mother was not well or she would not have been in Wichita in the Intensive Care Unit, but I hadn't been allowed to see her since arriving at the hospital. There were rules regarding minimum age.

In fact, I had not seen my mother since the night my father took her to the hospital in Great Bend, and I didn't know much about her condition. I was not overly alarmed even when they moved her to Wichita; my mother had experienced many health problems in my lifetime, some quite severe (on one occasion even warranting the Catholic ritual of last rites). This was not foreign territory for our family, holding vigil in a hospital family waiting room and this no doubt was reflected in my reluctance to believe what my family was telling me of her current condition.

However, this day was much different from any other that I had experienced. On this day a priest would tell a boy that his mother was going to die.

"I'm only..."(...in the hell?)

On this day a boy would have to come to terms with the imminent death of a parent. On this day a boy would lose part of the innocence that each child possesses, innocence lost much too early. On this day a boy would begin the struggle for an emotional survival that would lead him in directions that would fill him with doubt and pain for much of his life. This journey would begin on the roof of a Kansas hospital in May of 1973 and would not end for nearly twenty years.

Obviously, the death of a parent is one of the toughest experiences anyone can go through; to a child it is especially devastating. Children don't truly understand death nor do they wish to.

"Human!..." (where the hell did that come from??)

I had been to funerals; however, those had been grandparents, great uncles, and aunts; they seemed like surreal affairs, and I remembered forever the smell of death in the funeral homes. In some ways they were social events for me and my cousins to catch up on the latest family gossip and have fun playing games. However, this funeral would be different, much different.

I really don't know at that time how normal or different I was in relation to other children. I think it would have been safe to say that I was not as strong as many of my peers, certainly not physically and probably not even mentally.

"Damn it Jim! I'm only human!"

So there it was, the first time I remember thinking that crazy, quirky phrase. Why in the hell one's brain hooks into some dumb-ass phrase from a *Star Trek* show from God knows how many years ago is totally without explanation. Probably because I heard it executed with such grace by Bones to Captain Kirk so many times on that particular series over the years. But for whatever reason, ever since then when things get too crazy and I feel I'm on the fringe of sanity, I start to repeat this phrase to myself periodically, sometimes repeatedly. The weirder life gets, the more I seem to repeat it.

The repeating of those six seemingly harmless words in my mind that seemed to fire as randomly as any of the other meaningless pulses that go through one's mind millions of times a second, might well have been my first signal that I was going to be fighting for my sanity through the process of my mother's death. A battle that I knew I could win, but I had to play my cards just right, and keep them very close to the vest.

Even at a young age one strength I possessed—and still possess to this day—is that of knowing what I can handle and what I cannot. That strength would be both my salvation and my curse as the next week progressed.

...everyone in the family was gone from the waiting room. My dad was with my mom, Ron and Linda had gone across the street to a pharmacy shopping for a few essentials with my aunt; they were badly in need of a break.

As I sat alone, I could not help but look at the door to the intensive care unit. I tried not to dwell on it and my decision, but it was compelling to me. On the other side of that door lay my mother spending her last days, her last hours on earth.

My mother was fading and so was my last chance to see her alive one last time, to say my final goodbye. At one point I even mustered the spirit to walk down the hall toward the door, counting the steps along the way...

6, 7, 8...The hospital staff and my father had said "just go in that door if you change your mind, the desk nurse will arrange the visit immediately" (the emphasis on immediately once again signaling that time was short for such a decision to be made).

11, 12, 13...Damn it Jim! I'm only human! Damn it Jim, I'm only human, Damn it Jim...human, only human...only...

16, 17...And there it was, the door...

But it was not to be...I couldn't manage the strength to open it, let alone the courage to go inside.

The First Corridor

The first major test came almost immediately. The hospital would waive the age requirements if I wanted to see my mother in her final days. My brother and sister had gone in at least once, each time for a short visit in accordance with the regulations of the Intensive Care Unit. Now the priest and my father were telling me that I could see her as well.

Almost immediately I made the decision that I could not handle this challenge, to see my mother and have to say goodbye in person was more than I could bear. I felt as if I was hanging on to my sanity with a thread...this I could not do. My father, the priest, my brother, and my sister were supportive of my decision and did not pressure me to do otherwise. They just gave me an open invitation to let them know if I changed my mind.

As the hours progressed we waited. My dad, brother, and sister visited when allowed. I did not. As I look back now the distance from the waiting room to the intensive care entrance was comparable to the distance from the front door of the Ellinwood Hospital to the room my uncle would occupy almost seventeen years later. But as a thirteen-year-old boy, I looked at that hallway and it seemed miles long with treacherous hurdles and a very steep incline. At the prospect of that walk, my body seized with fear and trepidation. Even at this relatively young age I felt like a coward and that I was betraying and abandoning my mother in her final hours. In part, that feeling has never left—and may never leave—my soul.

While I still believe that I did what I needed to do to keep myself whole at that time, I obviously wonder as I write this book what would have been the impact had I gone in to see my mother. Would I have found peace? Or would it have been too much for me to handle? I will never know the answer. I can only imagine.

THE PASSING

The day my mother passed away seems as surreal now as it did that day thirty plus years ago. I can smell the room, I can hear the clock, I can see the nervous glances of our family and hear the small chatter trying to fill the silence. Our family knew what was coming; we knew why we were assembled. When the news was delivered, we all kept it together. Until the councilor from the hospital came in to give my dad my mother's wedding rings.

He started to disintegrate; I can still see him melt, crying, looking completely helpless. As horrifying as it was for a boy to see his rock begin to crumble, it was perfectly natural for this to happen because at the exact instant that my brother, sister, and I lost our mother, my father lost the love of his life.

As the day passed into dusk and as dusk passed into night, and as our tortured consciousness finally transitioned to a respite in the form of sleep, my two worlds started their headlong journey toward each other. These two remarkable life events, my mother's death and the inability of a young boy to take the walk down that long hospital corridor, would rapidly move toward a collision with a future death and a future corridor. A convergence of events that in hindsight seemed almost destined to occur and in many ways would forever change the way in which I view the world.

THE BLACK AND THE DARKNESS

There is much about the day of the funeral I do not remember. Actually as I think back on it, much of it is still a fog. I do remember my feeling of relief when I found out it was going to be a closed casket service. I had fallen ill from the flu shortly after my mother's death and my father had theorized that part of what had made me ill might have been psychological, the fear of seeing my mother in the coffin. If there is one thing I am thankful for in relation to these events it is that I cannot picture what my mother looked like in that coffin. When I remember her, my only memories are of her in life and for that I am forever thankful.

I don't remember going into the church with my family. I don't remember the sermon. What I do remember with exact clarity is the moment my sight abandoned me. I remember the light leaving the church gradually and the strange sensation of holding my hand up directly in front of my face and not being able to see it. I remember sitting back in the pew and telling my dad I was blind. I remember my Uncle Clayton taking me tenderly down the isle and out of the church into the fresh air, and my fear that I'd never see again. All of this is vividly burned into my memory.

I also recall thinking to myself how odd it was that I had not been able to cry since my mother's death. From the time the priest told me my mother was going to die, to the actual meeting in which they said she had passed away and even up to the funeral. Not a tear. I remember feeling this helpless sensation that if I started to cry I would never stop, that insanity would take my consciousness like a thief in the night and it might never be returned. Not here, not now, safer not to cry.

Damn it Jim! I'm only human…
Damn it Jim! I'm only ….

THE SEARCH FOR MEANING

There would be no deep soul searching after this funeral. The tears did not flow, not at the gravesite and not that night as I lay in bed. I still believe that the withholding of my emotions was what stole my sight for five minutes during my mother's funeral.

In this death there would be no search for meaning, none at all. There would only be a search for the next day...a day when the pain might subside. A search for life as it was, for innocence lost, a search for my father, his future and his salvation. These things would come in time, albeit painfully slowly and with much work.

Chapter 4

The Phoenix—The Growth through the Ashes

As I stood in front of my uncle's room and thought that the darkness of the moment might engulf me, I thought of another day and time when life seemed just as futile.

The time after the death of my mother, when I thought I would never find peace or purpose in my life again.

As I grasped for understanding, I recall thinking and reflecting on the Legend of the Phoenix" and wondering…if a Phoenix could emerge from the ashes to one day soar again, could I too somehow find a new meaning, a new direction to my life?

The Legend of the Phoenix has been around for centuries. The Phoenix is a supernatural creature, living for 1000 years. Once that time is over, it builds its own funeral pyre and throws itself into the flames. As it dies, it is reborn anew, and rises from the ashes to live another 1000 years.

—Internet Circulation

Rebirth and salvation would come for me in two forms. What went into this time of my life was a young boy who was afraid of his shadow; what slowly emerged was a confident, secure young man. A young man who, through the love and nurturing of others, was able to rebuild his self image, security, and his belief in God and life.

YOUR BROTHER'S KEEPER

The first and one of the most amazing blessings came soon after my mother's death. Without being asked and with no prodding, my brother Ron assumed the role of head of the household. He cooked, cleaned, laundered, and ran shuttles to keep the household going—all during his senior year in high school as well as what would have been his early years in college. He did this with little or no fanfare.

My sister Linda worked every hour she could to help fund her upcoming years at Kansas State University, as well as keep up with her studies at the community college in town.

And my father, while still struggling with the deep emotional issues of losing his wife, also needed to keep up with the demands of funding our household, as well as help put my sister through college.

Therefore, with the demands on my father and sister, much of the job (playing "mother hen") fell to my brother. Thankfully, he did it well and with no complaints. For this I have always been thankful and feel I can never totally repay what he gave up during that crucial period. I don't think I truly appreciated the sacrifices he made until I arrived at those ages myself.

THE STEP FAMILY

The next blessing came in the form of the stepfamily that was about to enter my life. It became evident fairly soon after my mother's death that my father was not wired to live without a spouse. I never took offense or felt threatened by this reality; he once told me that it was in fact a compliment to my mother. He said. "Larry, if a person has had a wonderful marriage, which I

did, he can never be truly happy living without that ever again."
Even at that young age, I could understand and appreciate his
sentiments on the matter.

When he began to date again, I was very supportive. I was
smart enough, even at the age of fourteen, to look past the popu-
lar myths about stepfamilies. Yes, no doubt Cinderella-like horror stories abound; however, I felt that this could be an opening
of a new chapter in our life. I felt a keen sense of promise as the
journey began.

The woman he found, whom I believe God delivered, came
in the form of a rather robust compact farm lady by the name
of Elizabeth Lula Rose (Betty) Hickey. Her husband had died a
couple of years earlier and she was very similar in circumstance
to my father—very lonely and in need of a new life partner. She
brought to the relationship a defined need for companionship
and a heart big enough to love another family.

Betty was a tough old bird with a very colorful personality.
She had arms as solid as brick from working on the farm and a
spirit just as formidable. She knew when to be tough and when
to soften up. And while we went through our rounds, she and I,
as near as I can tally she won every last one. In fact, she was the
toughness I needed to successfully extract my head out of my
nether regions. We emerged from these often challenging days
with a grudging respect that would eventually blossom into a
mature and unbreakable bond.

Betty had two daughters, Donna five years my senior and
Beverly one year younger than me. Donna moved out shortly
after Betty married my father, so I was not as close to her as I
might have been otherwise. Beverly, on the other hand, became
an instant soul mate; we were partners in crime and instant best
friends. We had both lost parents at about the same age and understood what each had experienced. I finally had in her a sibling close to my own age, a little sister. Later she would convince
me to leave my school and go to her high school, one of the
best decisions I ever made. And my stepsisters would eventually forge the same type of bond with my father that I did with
their mother.

Another bright spot was the extended family—the uncles,
aunts, cousins, and grandparents—they brought to the mix,

some of the most boisterous, in-your-face, and loving people you would ever want to meet. When I wanted to hide in my shell, they all physically and forcefully pulled me back out into the world. In this extended family I would get a grandmother, "Goldie" Cocker, I could call my own. She was a jewel of a woman who had a smile that could light the world and enough love to feed it as well.

Yes, this was just what the doctor ordered for me. What they got was a scared kid who lacked the confidence to face himself, let alone the rest of the world. And what emerged from this time was a confident, borderline cocky kid who thought he could whip the world, all in the span of three years.

Am I a believer in the potential of stepfamilies? You bet I am. There is no reason they cannot be extremely positive experiences. I have had many people say, and I would concur, that our two families have forged a closer bond than probably 80 to 90 percent of traditional families. We long ago dropped the "step" denotations when introducing each other, and we are all very proud of that fact.

This did not happen immediately, of course. It took years of diligence, hard work, and patience, much of it by my dad and stepmother, and a willingness to try something new by all of my siblings and myself. This indeed was the "growth through the ashes" that I had hoped for in my silent prayer.

Chapter 5

Death and the Transformation

I entered my uncle's room very quietly, so quietly, in fact, that he did not hear me enter. He was still in a light sleep. Knowing full well that this could be a temporary respite from his current situation I was reluctant to wake him. However, I knew this was my moment to be involved, to be an adult, to be a comfort to a loved one.

I gently reached down to touch Uncle Junior's hand. He did not wake immediately, so I gently grasped his hand and held it. His eyelids began to flutter, his eyes finally opened. After getting his focus he looked at me and smiled.

"Hello Larry, how are you?..."

SIBLINGS

In this section of the book, I will formally introduce you to my Uncle Junior. However, before I begin it is appropriate to expand a bit on the relationship between Junior and my mother, Barbara Jane Schartz. Much of what makes this story truly amazing is that a brother and sister reached across the void of time as well as that of life and death to teach this wondrous lesson to a nephew and a son. In part, this should not be surprising, when considering the closeness and the bond these two people shared.

My mother, as noted earlier, was part mother hen and part sister to Junior and his brothers. It is fair to say that my mother and Junior shared a special bond as children and young adults up until the time of my mother's death. I do not mean to take away from the relationship between her and her other brothers, but hers and Junior's bond was a special one.

I will not dwell on their relationship further at this point. Suffice it to say they were close and I believe it is important to understand the depth of their relationship to fully appreciate the lessons contained in my uncle's death.

THE MAN

Junior was not an extraordinary man by most measures. He married his wife Patricia at a fairly young age and they would go to work building a family of five kids. The kids shared a room with at least one sibling most of their childhood. Junior was definitely not afraid to use the rod to keep order, but within this sense of order was an underpinning of love, devotion, and respect.

They lived in the same frame bungalow on a quaint wooded street in Ellinwood for much of their married life. He was a very accomplished golfer, winning enough trophies to fill the main den of their house.

Even though Junior did not have much financially in their earlier years, he did whatever it took to provide for his family. My father and he were alike in that respect. Dad and my mother spent much time together with Junior and Pat. They often helped each other out, sharing game, fish, and even money back and forth, as well as other resources. Much of the time our family seemed to be marginally better off, probably because of two fewer mouths to feed and a bit more stable job situation, but both families plowed through the tough times together.

Junior was an avid hunter. As noted earlier in the book, part of the reason he hunted was not for sport but to provide food for the table. He did not make a big production of it, he just quietly did what he had to do to make ends meet. His wife Pat could make a feast of wondrous proportions with anything he could bag, and they were always quick to make the call and share it with our family or others in need.

As the years passed, the Schartz family's finances brightened. Junior was offered a partnership in the small manufacturing firm where he worked as general manager. With that partnership he obtained a security and a certain level of financial freedom his family hadn't known until then; however, they maintained the same residence their entire lives.

THE LAUGH

Giving someone a sense of who Junior was can not be adequately done without talking of his sense of humor. Junior knew and could remember more jokes than he could recount and he delighted in telling them. He could hold a group of people enthralled for hours and if you were bold enough to get into a joke telling contest, well…prepare to lose.

Yes…Junior had a knack for telling jokes; however, what made it especially rewarding was that he enjoyed them as much as anyone…then came the laugh. Junior had one of those endearing laughs. It wasn't annoying, it wasn't obnoxious, it was only infectious, and we all tolerated the occasional bad joke just to hear that laugh. Junior also had a tradition of doing the most hilarious chicken dance at wedding dances. He had to be somewhat motivated by enough libations (likely enough to kill a small mule), but once to that point…hang on. This was not the cheesy chicken dance many times seen performed by groups at weddings currently. This was one of his personal creations and it always brought down the house.

There was a lot of joy in that family, until that fateful day…

DEATH WARRANT

Early in the year of 1990 Junior got the news that his life would soon come to an end. Ironically, his illness was caused by the same business that had given him his first glimpse of financial security. The manufacturing company he partially owned manufactured pipe, fittings, and accessories. Unfortunately, asbestos filled the air. All who worked there were exposed; the asbestos was ingested and lay in wait like a ticking time bomb to claim its victims. One of those victims was my Uncle Junior.

My brother saw him approximately a week after my uncle received the diagnosis. He told Junior he was sorry to hear about his misfortune and asked if there was anything our family could do. "Just pray for me, Ron, nothing much else to do at this point. We don't deal the cards down here, we just have to play the hand we are dealt."

Shortly after that, Junior had exploratory surgery to see if anything could be done to extend his life for any meaningful amount of time...unfortunately, there was nothing to be done. Chemotherapy would not have much success and could diminish the quality of life that he had left. Junior led his family through the decision to make the best of the time he had, and not submit to the treatments.

The Hug

Junior spent the time he had left at home and around town. He also spent it getting his affairs in order. For his lawsuit against the asbestos company, video testimony had to be taken since he obviously would not be around to give it himself. He also went to work dividing personal belongings among his children and giving them pep talks to guide them through the rest of their lives.

Junior was admittedly not an outwardly affectionate man, at least not as much as he wished he had been. He tried to make up for that in his last weeks, telling his family of his love for them. He even gave long overdue hugs to each one; Junior had a design for what he wanted to accomplish during his final days of freedom, before being confined to a hospital bed.

Last Stay

When Junior went to the hospital for the last time, I imagine he knew it was such. I am sure he looked at each and every thing along the way, knowing it was probably for the last time.

However, he also knew that he had control of the decisions he would make until his last breath was drawn.

That last breath would be approximately a week after he would be admitted to the Ellinwood hospital, but what an extraordinary week it would be, and what a change it would make in any number of peoples lives. What a way to go out, to transition from one world to the next.

On the last night Junior was alive, he had an extremely interesting last request for his daughter Debbie. Debbie, a registered nurse, had been by his side much of that last week taking care of his needs as best she could.

Junior was very well aware that he was in the final stage of his life and that it would probably be a matter of hours; his voice was weak and his daughter had to listen closely to hear his request.

"*...save me...*"

"What?" Debbie asked confused.

"*...save me...*" Junior said again in a weakened voice.

"Dad, I am doing everything I can for you," Debbie implored, "but I can't save you."

"*...no,*" he said frustrated. This time he used physical motions to clarify his request, and Debbie heard what he was in fact attempting to convey.

"*Shave me,*" he asked again, this time mustering all the breath he could put behind his request.

Finally understanding, Debbie asked if everyone would clear the room for a few minutes. And then she tenderly shaved his face—the first and last time she would ever do so—a man so meticulous that he wanted to make sure he would look presentable and proper in his coffin as friends and relatives paid their final respects.

Part Two

Summer Corridors—The Life Lessons

The Summer of our life brings the corridors of
    colleges, dormitories or apartment buildings,
    corporate offices, law firms or manufacturing
    plants, honeymoon and birthing suites, and
    hopefully our first homes.
The corridors of power and influence, pride,
    and arrogance...doors flown wide open at
    our approach.
Corridors that will lead us to believe that all
    things are possible.

But what is life? Life is learning. Learning to love, hate, succeed, fail, forgive, to be arrogant and humble. And finally, learning how to let go of and give up all that we hold dear.

———

In the summer of my life, I would indeed believe that all things were possible. During my twenties and thirties I found a fix on life that not many my age would or possibly could, in part because of the unanswered issues surrounding my mother's death. However, largely due to the circumstances that would later surround my Uncle Junior's death, this period of my life was catapulted forward toward the identification of many questions...and more importantly toward many significant and astounding answers.

I spent this period of my early adulthood on many of the normal things that occupy a man in this stage of his life—marriage, starting a family, the first houses, and career development. But more importantly, I searched the depths of my soul and intellect for long-term answers to many of life's most challenging and intriguing questions.

You Got That?

This next part of the book will impart to you, my reader, much of what I learned on that all-encompassing journey. Some of what is to follow may not seem exactly germane to the topics at hand, but I will attempt to define at each stage how it does indeed fit with the mission at hand.

Furthermore, in the interest of making good on my rather bold promises, I will define at each stage of the book the promised answers to the rather dramatic and possibly life-altering questions...
- Why do we live?
- Why do we die?
- Why are doing both well vitally important.
- Why do bad things happen to good people?

To achieve the mission of this book, it is imperative that you do not go away without the answers (at least the possible answers) to these questions. Therefore, each section will be followed by a conclusion clearly identifying the answers contained in each section.

This may seem to be somewhat of an overemphasis and at times even borderline patronizing; I apologize in advance for that, however, I must take that risk.

Lesson 1

It's Not Just Your Death

As I drove home from Ellinwood after seeing Uncle Junior, the same thing happened each time. About two miles out of town, always at the same dirt road, I had to pull my vehicle over. To cry...

...to cry torrents, to unleash emotions too big for the death of an uncle, no matter how close.

This would last approximately five minutes each time. After the second time I began to ask myself where this was coming from. Yes, Junior was close and yes, I admired him a great deal, however that could not account for the intensity of my emotions. After the third time it happened, it suddenly came to me....

I was finally crying for my mother...

Before I begin, I must first apologize for and explain the name and topic of this chapter. It is very presumptuous of me to claim for anyone else even a partial ownership or stake in your eventual demise. However, in the interest of exploring my philosophies please allow me that latitude...if not for a while.

First, allow me to explain myself. When I say it is not just your death, I fully understand that death is a very personal and important event and each person should have ultimate control over his or her death just as over his life. There are those who write books giving advice on how to live your life. This book will offer advice on how to live your death. Yes live your death…

Just as there are many decisions in relation to living your life, there are a number of decisions concerning your death. Some mundane decisions would include:

- Type of funeral service.
- Type of burial (cremation or traditional).
- Where to be buried.
- What you want carved on your headstone.
- What church to conduct the last sacraments.
- The disbursement of your final estate.

These, however, are primarily actions taken shortly after your death. When I refer to living your death, I am talking about those things that happen shortly before your death—from the time an individual determines he is going to die in the foreseeable future, to the death itself.

Later in the book I will actually focus on what types of things a person should consider during this period of time. In this section I seek merely to educate people about the fact that decisions need to be made, and that those decisions will impact those around you.

Any Last Words?

Several things can be extremely important in relation to a person's last months alive. It is important to note, and may surprise you to realize, that your death may be one of the most important and significant events in some people's lives; your spouse, children, friends, and relatives for example. It is important to think about how we die and how it will impact those important to us. Here are some of the things that may be done preceding death to minimize the impact and even enhance the process for others:

- Determining the division of your final estate.
- Writing letters to those closest to you, expressing your feelings for them.
- Pre-planning your funeral service.
- Determining what fences (emotional, relational, and maybe physical) need to be mended while you are still able to do the work.

- Determining your spiritual needs before your passing.
- Thinking about how you want to present your life in your final months (the "life room").

These are only a sampling of the very important things that will need to be done preceding your death. This, however, pales in comparison to the most important thing that needs to be done. Talking.

Talking to anyone who will listen—and they will listen. People who rolled their eyes before will suddenly be willing and eager to listen. They will likely hang on every word. Why? Your words and counsel will be precious because they are now a finite resource. Therefore, it is extremely important to think in advance about what you want to say and who you want to say it to.

Will everyone suddenly agree with and do what you want? Not likely or even necessary, but they will remember what you say. The ghost of your words will be present with them long after you are gone, so make sure your words are timeless, and well thought out.

THE DEATH OF DYLAN EVERHART

What type of impact can someone's death have on another? We have all experienced death and each death has a different effect. Some we watch with a detached curiosity, perhaps an uncle or family friend that we didn't know very well. Some can have a traumatic impact on us such as the death of a spouse, child, or parent.

Make no mistake—each death impacts us in some way, whether it is positive or negative. It may seem strange that I suggest that death can have a positive impact and obviously in the short-term most deaths impact our lives negatively. However, in relation to this section of the book, I am not talking only about the short-term, I also refer to the long-term impact of a death.

Let me give you a couple of examples. I have a salesman who works for our company. Recently he and his wife tragically lost their son in an automobile accident. When I heard the news I felt numb and could barely breathe. Dylan was my son's age, only eight years old. How could this be?

Dylan died in a one-vehicle crash while driving with a relative who lost control of the car on a dirt road. Within seconds a precious life had been lost. This one was tough; how do you console the parents, the brother, sister, and grandparents? What can you possibly say to someone who has lost so much?

This was a life-changing event, one that helped move me toward the birth of this project. I stumbled through as best I could, I helped them financially and was there every step of the way, but I felt extremely ill equipped throughout the experience.

The only thing that made it much easier on everyone was the fact that this family did a wondrous job of going through the grieving process. They cried, hugged, and pulled everyone around them in and held on tight. Do they still miss their son and sibling every single day? Absolutely and desperately, but I believe they are doing so well now because of how well they proceeded through the grieving process those first few months.

I will never forget the day of the funeral. The service had to be moved to a bigger church in Salina and still there was not enough room. There were literally people hanging from the rafters. As I looked around that church I came to one definitive conclusion. This eight-year-old boy, whose life was cut much too short, was going to have as much impact over peoples' lives with his death, as if he had lived to be ninety years of age.

I don't know the impact his death had on others in that church, but I can tell you the effect it had on my life—it literally changed me forever. It made me a better parent and husband, and helped me further define an even healthier perspective in my life. I love a little deeper, I am a little more understanding, and I don't take nearly as much for granted since his death. The impact his death had on my life will never fade.

The Everhart family didn't realize it, but they were teaching me as well as many others how to get through a family tragedy. Teaching us how to go through a healthy grieving process, literally providing us a road map through some of the most treacherous terrain any of us might ever travel.

One important note: it is important to understand that Dylan did not die so that others and I could learn lessons such as these. As will be discussed later in the book there is randomness to tragic events such as this. I do not believe this death was God's will, and it was not necessary for this to happen for me or anyone else to learn and grow. Learning is many times a by-product of sad, devastating, incomprehensible tragedies; it is the unintended silver lining in the peripheral of these tragic circumstances.

My final word on this topic: there is a depth to my emotions that did not exist before Dylan Everhart's death. I, like so many others, desperately wish it had not come by way of this tragic experience, but his death's impact on the remainder of my life is undeniable.

The Military Death

Unfortunately it is played out too often all across the country. Soldiers in formal military dress get out of their vehicle and knock on the doors of unsuspecting loved ones to tell them their son or daughter has died for their country. Each and every instant brings tragedy and sadness to the families and friends affected.

In the immediate term these deaths are no doubt extremely tragic and negative events. However, in the long term these soldiers giving their lives helps to preserve the freedom and liberty we all hold dear, yet unfortunately too often take for granted. This is possibly the single best example of the long-term benefits that can come by way of death.

The Good Death

In this section of the book, I do not intend to undermine the challenges and trauma of death. But it could be so much more in many cases.

I don't intend to pretend to have all the answers. I also don't want to appear judgmental—each person's death and the process of dying is very personal. I can't guarantee you, as I write this book, how I will react when my time comes; I am sure I will battle the same issues anyone would.

We will all likely experience feelings of fear, resentment, anger, and hurt. This is part of an understandable and even desirable process (just as going through all of the stages of grief is considered healthy when another person dies). I believe if we don't go through a grieving process for the loss of our own physical life, we cannot come to terms with our death and help lead others through the process as well. Therefore, it is important how we deal with these feelings, fears, and anxieties, while keeping in mind the same issues exist for those closest to us at the same time.

I challenge each of us to be aware of the extraordinary things that can happen through the dying process. If we are aware of it, hopefully we do a little better job of planning for it and trying to ensure that in the long-term, our family will be all right. Ultimately I must ask myself, how can I **live my death** in a way that will provide for a **long-term positive impact on my family and loved ones?**

LIFE INSURANCE = PEACE OF MIND

There is no better way to provide for our families after our death than with life insurance. As obvious as that seems, too often people don't secure it. Imagine the peace of mind in knowing that after you are gone your family will be financially secure. Through life insurance, purchased at early- and mid-stages of our lives, we and our loved ones can have just that peace of mind.

CONCLUSIONS

This section of the book addresses two key questions, **why it is important that we die well** (just as we attempt to live well) and **why bad things happen to good people** (the death of Dylan Everhart).

We attempt to die well because our death can and likely will have an impact on those close to us, many times a dramatic impact on the rest of their lives. As in the case of Dylan's death, many of life's most powerful lessons, as well as our most profound emotional growth, may only come by way of tragic events in which bad things happen to good people.

Lesson 2

The "Forging" of Our Emotions

During the waning years of the depression in a small southeastern Idaho community, I used to stop by Mr. Miller's roadside stand for farm-fresh produce as the season made it available. Food and money were scarce and bartering was used extensively.

One particular day Mr. Miller was bagging some early potatoes for me. I noticed a small boy, delicate of bone and feature, ragged but clean, hungrily apprising a basket of freshly picked green peas. I paid for my potatoes but was also drawn to the display of fresh green peas. I am a pushover for creamed peas and new potatoes. Pondering the peas, I couldn't help overhearing the conversation between Mr. Miller and the ragged boy next to me.

"Hello Barry. How are you doing today?"
"H'lo, Mr. Miller. Fine, thank ya. Jus' admirin' them peas… sure look good."
"They are good, Barry. How's your Ma?"
"Fine, Gittin stronger alla' time."
"Good. Anything I can help you with?"
"No, Sir. Jus' admirin' them peas."
"Would you like to take some home?"
"No, Sir. Got nuthin' to pay for 'em with."
"Well, what have you to trade me for some of those peas?"
"All I got's my prize marble here"
"Is that right? Let me see it"

"Here 'tis. She's a dandy."

"I can see that. Hmmmm, only thing is this one is blue and I sort of go for red. Do you have a red one like this at home?"

"Not 'zackley… but, almost."

"Tell you what. Take this sack of peas home with you and next trip this way let me look at that red marble."

"Sure will. Thanks, Mr. Miller."

Mrs. Miller, who had been standing nearby, came over to help me. With a smile she said, "There are two other boys like him in our community, all three are in very poor circumstances. Jim just loves to bargain with them for peas, apples, tomatoes or whatever. When they come back with their red marbles, and they always do, he decides he doesn't like red after all and he sends them home with a bag of produce for a green marble or an orange one, perhaps."

I left the stand, smiling to myself, impressed with this man. A short time later I moved to Colorado, but I never forgot the story of this man, the boys, and their bartering.

Several years went by, each more rapid than the previous one. Just recently I had occasion to visit some old friends in that Idaho community and while I was there learned that Mr. Miller had died. They were having his viewing that evening and knowing my friends wanted to go, I agreed to accompany them.

Upon our arrival at the mortuary, we fell into line to meet the relatives of the deceased and to offer whatever words of comfort we could.

Ahead of us in line were three young men. One was in an army uniform and the other two wore nice haircuts, dark suits and white shirts…very professional looking. They approached Mrs. Miller, standing smiling and composed, by her husband's casket. Each of the young men hugged her, kissed her on the cheek, spoke briefly with her and moved on to the casket. Her misty light blue eyes followed them as, one by one, each young man stopped briefly and placed his own warm hand over the cold pale hand in the casket. Each left the mortuary, awkwardly, wiping his eyes.

Our turn came to meet Mrs. Miller. I told her who I was and mentioned the story she had told me about the marbles. Eyes glistening she took my hand and led me to the casket.

"Those three young men who just left were the boys I told you about. They just told me how they appreciated the things Jim 'traded' them through the years. Now, at last, when Jim could not change his mind about color or size...they came to pay their debt. We've never had a great deal of wealth of this world," she confided, "but right now, Jim would consider himself the richest man in Idaho."

With loving gentleness she lifted the lifeless fingers of her deceased husband. Resting underneath were three, magnificently shiny red marbles.

Moral: We will not be remembered by our words, but by our kind deeds. Life is not measured by the breaths we take, but by the moments that take our breath away.

W.E. Peterson
1975 Ensign Magazine

In many of the classes I teach, I read the preceding story and I must admit that I rarely get through it without my voice quivering and my eyes tearing up. I find this amazing in that I have read this story to over twenty-five classes of students; I must confess to the same level of emotion as I typed the story for this book.

What is it about this story that I find so intriguing? Obviously the moral is extraordinary and important in itself. However, it is the emotion that this story brings out in people that makes it such a powerful lesson. This story in fact touches the depths of many emotions—happiness, sadness, inspiration, admiration, shame, and indecision. Yes, even shame and indecision...would we have been as generous had we been in Mr. Miller's situation?

As I read this story in class and struggle to keep my own emotions somewhat in check, I find it intriguing to observe the reaction and the emotions of the students in the classroom. Most feel the power of the story. Many can identify with the man who shows such compassion for the boys and their families challenging situation. Very few can identify firsthand with the boy's situations however, because very few of us have had the actual experience of wondering where our next meal is coming from. Fortunately, most of us have been sheltered and protected by our families, governments, and social agencies from that stark reality.

This story hits at a fundamental level with most people; especially those who have a normal range of experiences and empathy for all of humankind. Initially, it brings us face to face with the reality that there will always, at any given time, be bad and unjust things taking place in the world. We further understand that no matter how hard we try to make the world just and fair, there will always be bad things happening to really good people. And finally, we understand that no matter how secure life seems for us currently, terrible, tragic, and maybe even horrific things might happen in our future.

When and if this happens, will we be able to find our own Mr. Miller, someone to help us through our darkest, most challenging days? Will we be able to be as brave and resilient as the boys in the story, and find a way through those challenges?

This story touches a range of issues and emotions that ring eternal. As I read and reread this story with its timeless message, each time experiencing different and unique emotions, I often times wonder what is next. What emotional dimensions are yet to be uncovered and explored in our time on this Earth...before we can be divine?

THE MECHANICS OF OUR EMOTIONS

As noted earlier in the book, my father's early career was that of a truck mechanic, a very good one, possibly one of the best in the state (in his day). Early in my business career I asked my father why it was necessary to run engines at a high rate of speed for an extended period of time after an engine overhaul was completed. My father told me that it is necessary to "seat" the engine, and went on to explain that "seating" the engine was the process of making sure the engine was performing at a high level and that all the seals were sealing properly. Furthermore, putting the engine under that kind of pressure early on actually helps to tighten it and make sure it will be able to function properly for an extended period of time under optimal loads.

I believe this example draws a good parallel in relation to what must take place with our emotions. To ensure that our emotions are developed and functioning properly it is necessary to "seat" them as well. Before we explore the mechanics of how this takes place, let us first examine why it is important that it happen at all.

EMOTIONS? ARE THEY IMPORTANT? WHY?

Are emotions important? Is it necessary that we develop a wide range of emotions in our lifetime? If so, why?

Probably not much controversy here, yes on all counts. I believe a wide range of emotions is necessary for us to be able to move to the next level in our journey, which I believe is to be divine and with God. A person must "seat" or "forge" his or her emotions, and this is only accomplished by putting emotions under pressure and strain, pulling them, pushing them, heating them, cooling them, taking them to extreme highs and then lows. As we do all of this over a lifetime, our emotions grow and expand, and more importantly we identify and develop new ones.

It is my theory that for us to be divine and worthy to go to the final level and be with our creator, we must first engage and even initialize our full range of emotions. Both fortunately and unfortunately there is only one way this must and can be accomplished; it is necessary for us to personally experience most if not all of the emotions relevant to the human experience. Let us pause for a moment and identify at least a partial listing of the emotions that one can experience in a lifetime:
- Love
- Hate
- Joy
- Sadness

- Envy
- Lust
- Fear
- Ecstasy
- Anxiety
- Depression
- Despair
- Pride
- Shame
- Humility
- Terror

I think we would all agree that this is not a complete listing. A much larger list could be compiled if needed or desired. If it is truly necessary that we experience most if not all of these emotions over the course of a lifetime to become worthy of moving to the next level, it would in fact take a large range of life events to bring about the emotional experiences necessary. Life events such as:

- Births
- Deaths
- Tragedies
- Divorce
- Catastrophic events
- Glory
- Scandals
- Marriages
- Graduations
- Winning
- Losing
- Success
- Failure

Once again the list could go on and on. The important note is that it might take many of these types of events to bring about sustained emotional growth over a lifetime. I know it seems ironic to think of a tragedy in your or another person's life bringing about emotional growth, however that is exactly what happens.

Building Our "Emotional Muscle"

Let's parallel for a moment the building of physical muscle with that of the construction of our emotional structure. Most people understand and would acknowledge that for us to build physical muscle mass, it is necessary to strain the muscle. In fact, it is not only necessary to strain the muscle, it is actually necessary to tear or partially destroy it so it will grow back stronger than it was before.

This same principle may well hold true in relation to building our emotional muscle. It must be strained, torn and even partially destroyed before it can be reconstructed and made stronger than it was before. This straining and tearing of our emotions comes in many forms, some of them subtle, some of them rather dramatic and even traumatic. The following are two examples; one especially dynamic in my life and one fairly understated in comparison that still had a very substantial impact on the growth of my emotions.

The Birth of Hillary

I still remember with extreme joy the day my wife came into our bedroom and showed me the early pregnancy test that verified that we were pregnant with our first child. We were both ecstatic because we had been through so much stress and heartbreak along the way. My wife had had two surgeries early in our marriage and later had to have another to remove adhesions that had built up as a result. The surgeries had taken a toll on her reproductive system and she later had yet another surgery to address these issues. It took approximately four hours and came with no guarantees of success, offering us only a small chance of conceiving a child naturally.

For three years after that surgery we traveled on a perilous journey of extreme highs and lows—unfortunately many more low points than high. It was an emotional roller coaster full of dashed hopes but our continued goal of a family kept us going. So that day when my wife finally had confirmation that our dreams would be realized, we were full of hopes for the future.

The pregnancy was rather uneventful. We both had fun going through the natural progressions. First hearing the heartbeat and later seeing activity and movement within her stomach, some of which was reminiscent of a B-grade horror movie. At times it seemed as though the baby inside might explode through the stomach lining and into the world.

As we went through those experiences together, I never fully shared something with my wife that was a very real concern for me. I didn't feel paternal. I didn't feel that I was gaining the same passion, excitement, and instincts for parenthood that I was watching my wife experience. At times I was extremely concerned and borderline terrified about this lack of feelings and emotion, so much so that I wondered if I would be able to adequately bond with and fall in love with our baby.

It seemed as if the baby took forever to arrive. The wondering whether it was a boy or a girl, and the fear and anticipation of being a parent, built with each passing day. Then came the day of the birth. My wife's labor was very uneventful—of average length and fairly natural in how the stages progressed. I felt at ease and was very excited at all that was taking place. Still the fear lingered.

Those fears started to melt away in the early morning hours of December 16, 1990 when I first saw my daughter begin to emerge. It completely disappeared when I saw her in her entirety for the first time, and it was replaced with an emotion I had never experienced before when the nurse handed her to me to hold for the first time. It was as if someone had flipped a switch and illuminated an entire set of emotions heretofore hidden from me.

When I looked into my daughter's eyes for the first time, all doubt and trepidation disappeared, replaced with a commitment and passion to take care of her and my family for the rest of their life. It came fully with an understanding...what I was before that night now fell a distant second to the priorities that would now be most important.

With this life-changing event, my life and the way I viewed the world changed forever.

The Boys and the Drain Pipe

The previous example was obviously a major life-changing event. Many times, however, emotions can be engaged and developed as a result of some relatively minor influences. A short while back I was scanning my email account at my business. An email from a friend of mine was entitled "The Year in Pictures," a collection of some of the year's best photographs. There were about twenty pictures in all and they were all quite remarkable; however, one photo in particular impacted my life significantly.

It was toward the end of the list of photos and depicted a scene that tore at my heart and soul. Two young boys (approximately ten years of age, the same age as my son Brantley at the time) lying in a four foot tall drain pipe, in the background of which was the ravished landscape of a poverty stricken section of New Delhi, India. Both of the boys were asleep, angelic, and huddled in the drain pipe trying to escape the scorching midday heat. They both could just have easily been at a sleepover with my own son.

Why did this picture have such an impact on my life? I, like so many others, see images like this nightly on the television newscasts, many pictures of many kids and families, many in situations just as dire and desperate as this.

So why this picture? Why this impact? Why now?

After thinking at great length about these questions, the answer finally came to me and seemed relatively obvious in retrospect. The same picture or types of pictures would have a totally different impact on your life dependent on the life experiences you have to that point. For instance, if I didn't have children the picture might not have impacted me with such force, or with any at all. Additionally, had my son been four instead of the approximate age of the boys in the photo, it would likely have made a difference. Finally, a person will react to stimuli such as this photo differently at the age of forty-five than at twenty-five.

Many times we are incapable or not ready to develop many of life's emotions until later in our lives. We often feel guilty about that fact but in the final analysis, it is an extremely natural growth process. I could not have possibly reacted to and experienced that photo with the same depth of emotion until I had developed an emotional foundation (in this case the fact that I had children, one of whom was the same age and gender as the boys in the photo). Just as it takes a foundation to build a house, it takes a foundation of preliminary emotions to build the other emotions that need to be developed in a lifetime.

A Final Thought on Emotional Development

I want to conclude this section of the book by noting what probably seems somewhat obvious. There are several different ways to develop the same types of emotions. Am I trying to say in my example (the birth of Hillary) that you have to be a parent or you will be emotionally under-developed? Absolutely not, I am sure there are any number of ways to develop the same emotions I described, by way of other experiences.

You may not experience the joys of raising children, but you will experience many other things that we, who are parents, have given up. One set of experiences is not necessarily better than another they are simply different. The most important factor is to challenge yourself to experience life from as many different viewpoints as possible, giving yourself the best opportunities to develop your emotions as fully as possible.

When we are experiencing tragedy or challenges in our lives, part of the long-term good that could emerge is the development of and a newfound depth to our emotional foundation. Be vigilant and attempt to look for the light that might well emerge from life's darkest moments.

Conclusions

This section of the book could be deemed "ground zero" in terms of accomplishing the mission at hand. This part of the book deals extensively with all four questions.

Why do we live? Only through experiencing life can we truly develop our emotions. We must experience all life has to offer, the good and bad, the happy and sad, tragedy and triumph.

Why do we die? Many times it is only through the experience of death and tragedy that we can develop the depths of our emotions. Furthermore, we cannot fully develop our emotions without the scarcity of time.

Why is doing both well (living and dying) vitally important? Because both are absolutely necessary to fully develop our emotions and enable us to be divine.

Why do bad things happen to good people? Through injustice we find compassion, through unfairness we find the depths of our ability to empathize with our fellow man.

The following intriguing questions occurred to me through the writing of this chapter. Was it necessary for Jesus to initialize his emotions by experiencing the joys and tragedies of life? Was his emotional development (the "seating" of his emotions") finalized in the final twenty-four hours of his life? Obviously it is just speculation and possibly even presumptuous to even ask the question, however I could not get it totally out of my mind while constructing this part of the book.

Lesson 3

Know You Are Driving...

Two elderly women, both in their seventies, began their day of shopping with a drive across town on a pleasant afternoon. Sylvia, the passenger, was enjoying the seemingly uneventful drive until noticing that Ethel, the driver of the car sped through a red light at the first intersection they encountered without slowing down or looking either way for oncoming traffic. Sylvia became concerned, however upon reflection she talked herself out of what she had just witnessed. She must have imagined the whole thing.

About the time she was able to convince herself that it could not have happened, Ethel again sped through a second red light just a few blocks later. Once again she did not slow down and did not appear to look either way before entering the intersection.

Again Sylvia was contemplating her own recollection, trying to determine if she could have once again misinterpreted what had just happened. Upon coming to the conclusion that she did not imagine either incident, she was busily trying to determine a delicate way to bring the subject up to Ethel, when suddenly the car and driver once again sped through an intersection, red light on and no sign of slowing the car down or looking for other vehicles.

Finally Sylvia mustered up the nerve to broach the subject with Ethel. "You know Ethel," she said, "when you went through the first light I really thought I imagined it, when you went through the second light I must admit I questioned my own faculties, however after you went through this last red light I knew it had happened and it was time for me to speak up."

"What in the world are you doing running three consecutive red lights, without looking or so much as slowing down. Are you trying to get us killed?"

"Oh my," said Ethel in an unsteady, panicky voice...."Am I driving?"

———

This rather humorous story highlights a common problem in people of all ages and backgrounds. They do not realize they are driving. They do not realize they are leading others, modeling behaviors that others may choose to emulate. They do not recognize when people are looking to them for leadership or guidance about how to live their lives.

Interestingly enough and as unlikely as it might seem, one of the principal lessons I learned through the experiences detailed in this book are in relation to leadership. Not only understanding better what leadership is and what different forms it takes, but also the importance of good leadership. Leadership that is **worthy of followers**.

ARE YOU WORTHY OF FOLLOWERS?

The first question people must ask themselves before seeking leadership opportunities is are they worthy of followers? Will you be able to lead people in a worthwhile direction they should aspire to?

Before we start on that journey, we must address preliminary issues concerning the state of one's own life. This can best be accomplished by asking some simple but revealing questions.

- Are you doing a good job leading and managing your own personal life?
- Do you understand yourself, your needs and your desires?

- Do you have a clear understanding of where you are headed with your life?
- Do you genuinely feel good about yourself and the direction your life is headed?

If you cannot provide an answer in the affirmative to most if not all of these questions, you should consider whether leadership is for you at this time.

Answering no to some of these questions may not preclude all leadership prospects. If it is a beginning or entry-level leadership position and the stakes are relatively low, it may in fact be ideal. Everyone has to start somewhere and learn from the ground up. Civic groups, churches, and many other volunteer organizations are great training grounds for people to develop not only their leadership skills but also life skills.

Another somewhat controversial avenue is a marketing organization such as Amway, Mary Kay etc. Even though many of us (myself included) are somewhat annoyed when we are called by their representatives, they do have value in relation to the opportunities they provide for learning. They teach people valuable business and life skills, and they are solid, low risk ways to learn the fundamentals of business and leadership.

If a person cannot answer yes to the questions posed above and does not have the life skills necessary, he/she should slow down and "back fill" his life. **It is crucial to understand that leadership is an earned privilege, not a guaranteed right.** You must first know that you can lead your own life in positive and rewarding directions before asking or expecting others to follow. Before earning the privilege of leadership.

Parents as Dependents

Knowing you are ready to lead can be evidenced in a couple of different forms. First is personal responsibility, both financial and moral. My father has told me over the years that he would never have a person managing a division or department of his business that could not first manage his own life. He noted that if a person can't manage his own finances, how could he possibly manage hundreds of thousands and maybe even millions of dollars for a company.

I think this extends to the topic at hand; if a person cannot manage his finances, how can he legitimately lead others in any capacity at all? This does not mean that a person who has had financial problems cannot ever be worthy to lead others. But he has to first get his own house in order before assuming such responsibilities.

The second area that must be solid before leading others is the morality and trustworthiness of the individual. Entire books have been written on this subject so I don't plan to belabor the point. However, it is noteworthy that if an individual does not know where his own moral compass points, he will lead his life in very erratic, unpredictable, and often times destructive ways. These types of people do not need to take anyone else along for the ride.

A good friend of mine who had mentally and emotionally underdeveloped parents noted it was a very sad day for him, at the age of fifteen, when he figured out that he had likely surpassed his parents in terms of maturity and responsibility. Furthermore, he knew then that he would probably be leading and taking care of them, in one form or another, for the rest of their lives. Unfortunately, he was correct. His parents have always been in trouble—they jump from one financial or emotional crisis to another, their lives are in constant turmoil, and they count on his help bailing them back out of trouble when it predictably arrives.

He was fortunate in that he identified relatively early in his life that this was not the type of life he wanted to emulate for his own family. He is a college graduate, has a great family, and is a business executive. He has been extremely successful and was able to break his family's destructive cycles. His parents had no idea they were "driving the car," or if they did they were too mentally incapacitated to drive it safely, and certainly had no business carrying passengers.

LEADING YOUR CHILDREN

I think most would agree that there is no greater responsibility than that of leading your children. Unfortunately, though most of us agree with this statement, fewer and fewer of us are actually fulfilling our responsibility in this respect. Increasingly we are trying to be our kids' best friends, their confidants, and in some cases even trying to be part of their social circle.

While not all of this is bad, it does not excuse us from the responsibilities of being parents first and foremost. This means defining standards, enforcing rules, and meting out discipline if those rules are not followed.

I readily acknowledge that this discussion is borderline patronizing. Before digging in your heels, look around next time you are at the mall. How many twelve-, thirteen-, and fourteen-year-old kids do you see hanging out unsupervised, some openly flirting and kissing with other teens many times much older than themselves? Those kids' parents are not leading their children, they are appeasing them and allowing them to do what they want. This relieves the parents of having to deal with the kids and disrupt their own lives.

Whoa Bessie!

When my daughter went from the sixth to the seventh grade, we had an-eye opening experience. Although it was just one grade, it was going from grade school to middle school and an entirely different building. Almost overnight things changed; the topics of conversation between her and her friends turned to boys, and we noticed racier language and references to sexual topics. Some of her friends started to hang out at the mall unsupervised and were beginning to go on dates. One of my daughter's friends was encouraging my daughter to call boys and try to line up dates for the two of them, and my daughter was actually prepared to make the call on one occasion until we intervened.

After about one month of middle school, my wife and I were reeling, wondering what our reactions should be as well as what positions we should take. We talked one evening while out for a long walk in the neighborhood and agreed that we should each do some research and talk to other parents before determining our next moves. We knew we needed to act quickly so that we did not allow destructive patterns to formulate and take hold in our daughter's life.

After much research on the Internet and talking to many parents, most of whom had successfully raised good kids, our positions became clear. We decided that we would not allow our daughter to date until she was sixteen, and then it would be defined by rules and guidelines until she was eighteen.

Now…to break the news. What would be her reaction?

My wife and I decided I should have the talk with her, and I decided to have the discussion on an extremely long walk in our neighborhood on a Saturday morning. It was a wonderful day, we were both in a good mood, and my daughter was under no stress. I told her of her mother's and my decision on the matter, and I stressed that we had many experiences she was yet to have and that she would need to trust our judgment on the matter. I defined the parameters of our decision and she asked a few questions. She told me she understood and that she would abide by our decision and….that was it! No fighting, no arguing, nothing.

As we continued our walk that day, I sensed that Hillary understood that we had in fact conducted extensive research on the topic and arrived at a logical, caring decision that took her best interest into account. I could sense that day and even past that day that she felt proud to have parents who cared enough to intervene and make rules that would help guide her life in positive directions. I even overheard her almost boasting to her friends that she could not date until she was sixteen because her parents would not let her.

Will it go as easy for everyone? Surely not. But we were dug in for the fight no matter what. We felt strongly concerning this position and the research backed it up, not only firm published research but also the opinions and experiences of people who had raised very good kids. It has been almost two years since that talk and not once has my daughter put pressure on us to waiver from our decision. We do allow her to go places with friends, but those outings are structured and chaperoned.

Despite what kids say and some parents conveniently choose to believe, kids want to be led. Kids want parents who are good role models. They want parents they can be proud of and emulate in their own lives.

The Mission Statement

How can the pitfalls be avoided? Know yourself and understand your strengths, weaknesses, responsibilities, and obligations—not only to yourself but also to those you might lead. This is best accomplished by developing what is known as a mission statement, a statement that defines who you are and what you stand for, something that anyone who might follow you can review and see if you are worthy of following. Mission statements can and should be utilized for a business, personal use, or even a project. I have included examples of my personal statement as well as the one I did for this book.

Yes, I developed a mission statement for this book because as I began to develop the project that evolved into this book, it became evident that the most challenging part was going to be keeping the book focused and relevant to the topic. How would I accomplish this if I did not develop a mission statement defining the project and what I wished to accomplish? The following is that mission statement.

It is my goal in writing this book to write a manual for dealing with some of the most difficult and challenging issues and times that any of us will experience, the death of a loved one. Additionally I hope to share the many lessons I have learned from the experiences in relation to the deaths of my mother and uncle.

I do not write this book to glorify my family or myself; I will utilize real people and life experiences because they are relevant to the topic and can help develop and illustrate the points I am trying to make. Through this book I hope to help people learn, hope, heal, and eventually "finish well." Help them to live their life and their death to the fullest and become a leader worthy of followers.

Some of the initial elements of a good mission statement involve detailing what the end is that you would expect to achieve and how you intend to accomplish it. Saying what is and is not acceptable within the scope of this project has helped keep me focused. Many times during the writing of this book

I threw out entire sections because they did not fit the stated mission statement.

The following is my personal mission statement. By reading this you will hopefully have a better idea of my ability to lead, especially in relation to the topics discussed within this project.

I see each day as a clean slate, a fresh chance to write a new script and seize new opportunities. I value life's experiences and seek to learn and grow from each one. In my daily endeavors, I avoid neither risk nor responsibility. Nor do I fear failure, only lost opportunity.

I am a responsible spouse and parent; I give priority to these roles. I value differences in people and their perspectives and view them as strengths. I seek to build win – win relationships with family, friends, and business associates. Furthermore, I ascribe to the theory of abundance and believe we should strive to continue to "grow the pie" so that all can prosper.

In my profession, I see myself as a servant-leader who is responsible for results. I strive to act with courage, consideration, and discretion. I pledge to make decisions based on business and personal principles with an emphasis on fairness, not on politics, popularity, or expediency. While it is certain that not all of my decisions will be correct, I readily acknowledge and take responsibility for each and every one.

My goal is to live my life defined by the following personal and business principles; these principles shall serve as the framework for my decision making process:

- Respect for all types of people, realizing that everyone has worthwhile contributions to make.
- Respect for and commitment to family, realizing that the cultivation of sound families is the basis for a flourishing society.
- Respect for and active participation of intellectual and spiritual knowledge, realizing that knowledge comes in many different forms.
- Sound business practices based on honesty and integrity, realizing that an end result of good business is people who can grow socially, economically, and spiritually.

- Physical fitness, realizing that without this all else can be considered futile.
- A sound perspective and a good sense of humor, realizing that laughter is the key to a healthy perspective and lends itself to mental and physical health.

In closing, I choose to focus on the positive, to work within my circle of influence to impact things I can change. By doing this, I will increase my circle of influence and reduce my circle of concern.

Many people avoid writing mission statements because they are intimidated at the prospect of having to live up to them. Rest assured, many times we will not. A mission statement is what we aspire to be, <u>who we are on our best day</u>. Although many times we will fall short of the lofty standards we have set, it is still important that we set them. Mission statements define who we are, what is important, and what we are (and are not) willing to do to achieve our goals in life.

I will not belabor the technical aspects of writing a mission statement—many others have done extensive work on this topic, some of the best by Stephen Covey in his book *The 7 Habits of Highly Effective People*.

CONCLUSION

The primary question answered in this chapter is **why is it important that we do both well (living and dying)?** Very simply, because we are leading our families, our children, and our friends, up to and including the time of our death. They are watching and learning.

My son and I recently visited my Great Aunt Ada for the holidays (she will be highlighted further at a later point in the book), who had just a week earlier celebrated her ninety-second birthday. As we watched her during our visit we were amazed at how sharp her mind was. She insisted on cooking us lunch, and later that day even went to a museum with us. We offered several times through the day to help her with tasks, even insisting that we take her to lunch. She would not hear of it.

She was slow, to be sure. But she plodded determinedly, telling me that it was important for her to keep moving and keep working her muscles or they will get softer and cease to function properly. She told me of other little tricks that she employed, for instance she plays solitaire in the kitchen when she is cooking so she doesn't forget the food is in the oven.

If I am blessed to reach those advanced ages, I will remember the lessons I learned from my great aunt that day as she exhibited firsthand how to live with dignity, determination, and grace.

Lesson 4

The Importance of Family

After parking my vehicle in front of the Ellinwood hospital, I became aware that the parking stall I had chosen was directly in front of my uncle's room.

I sat frozen, momentarily watching what was going on inside the room. I could actually see it quite clearly even through the translucent shades.

The couple of lights on in the room threw a dim glow throughout the space. Inside was my first cousin Debbie, a daughter taking care of her father in his final day of life. She was in constant motion moving about the room, doing this and that to make him more comfortable. Being a registered nurse she could do things for him that most people were unaware of. It was obviously very tough on her, but it was at the same time a labor of love to keep her father as comfortable as possible in his final hours.

I asked her that evening how she could go about her work with him and remain so calm and seemingly together. She just shrugged her shoulders and said...

"He's my dad..."

When I embarked on this life-defining project, I defined one uncompromising standard for this book. Call it my mantra if you will, a simple statement that hung above the desk in my den where I did the majority of my writing. This simple, non-negotiable proclamation read...**"First speak the truth."**

With this standard as my backdrop, I engage in this section of the book at the risk of coming across as preachy, patronizing, controversial, or even pious. While this is obviously not my ultimate goal (and actually my fear), I will take that risk because I believe what I say to be true. I also acknowledge that to many of you this section may strike you as fairly obvious. Unfortunately those who fall into this category are an ever-shrinking minority in our society.

DIVORCE

Before I begin, let me make a needed disclaimer to all that will follow. Divorce is not always bad. Some marriages are not healthy and need to end, for the sake of not only the couple themselves but ultimately for the children involved. Therefore, I do not mean to lay guilt at the doorstep of all those who have or will divorce. Some women and even some men are married to mentally or physically abusive people, and they should not continue in these relationships out of a blind sense of obligation to their marriage vows or the children involved.

I also have somewhat torn emotions concerning couples who stay together for the children's sake (until they are past a certain age). As noble as this may seem, it needs to be examined very closely with an understanding in relation to how it will work and be communicated. It may be best, if this course is decided upon, that parents communicate the situation to the children, possibly not sharing a bedroom so it is clearly understood by all parties.

I have a good friend whose parents lived the masquerade of a normal married life, fooling friends, family, and kids. However, when the marriage ended after the last kid was out of high school, it came as a complete shock to the then young adults. My friend told me rather dejectedly, "When I look at family pictures

(from my youth), I feel like we were all living an elaborate lie."
As evidenced by this example, divorce may not always be the
worst thing that can happen.

Additionally, I would like to reemphasize that I am a firm believer in the potentially positive experience of stepfamilies. As noted earlier in this book, I am the product of a wonderful experience
in a non-traditional family. The relationships developed within our
stepfamily are among my most treasured family bonds.

On The Other Hand...

That being said, I do believe that many marriages could be
salvaged if the people involved would put the needs of their
family's long-term future over their immediate short-term needs.
Parents often fail to take into account the impact of divorce, particularly on the children they have both agreed to bring into the
world—not only the immediate shock but also the extended impact of the breakup.

The immediate shock is obvious. In many cases it turns the
kids' worlds upside down. Everything they thought they knew
is proven to be false, and all they thought was stable is now
unstable. This can have an immediate impact on family relationships and even personal relationships with friends. In itself this
is devastation enough; now let's continue to follow it through.
What is the long-term impact on the rest of their lives?

THE GREATEST LESSON

Let me illustrate by sharing an experience from my collegiate days. I was involved in a serious relationship with a young
woman I had met during my junior year. We got along very well
and dated for approximately six months. She was a very fun-
loving, intelligent, and dynamic woman. However, as the relationship progressed I noticed some disturbing patterns. If we
got into a dispute or even a fight, she was very quick to want to
break up. I was always the peacemaker and had to scramble to
patch things up. I did this several times because I cared for her
and about the relationship.

As the months went on and I learned more about her and her family life, it became evident that her parent's bitter divorce years earlier had left severe scars on her that were potentially impacting her ability to commit to a relationship. The problems continued and escalated to a point where it became apparent to me that this was not going to be a healthy bond. At one point when she wanted to end the commitment, I finally let it go, determined that it was the best thing to do.

Why did I know this? Because I had three wonderful teachers in relation to what constituted a healthy loving relationship, my mother, my father, and my stepmother. I had witnessed firsthand what commitment was, I knew what true love looked like, and I knew that if you truly knew how to commit and you truly loved another person, you didn't just walk away—you fought for that love and the relationship.

The point to this story is that I knew all of this because I had three parents who had modeled it for me. My ex-girlfriend tragically did not know it, recognize it, or know how to accomplish it because her parents did not teach it to her. Does this mean that people who come from this type of messy divorce cannot be happily married? Certainly not! But it does mean that they could have lower odds and a tougher time than someone who has seen a good marriage work. In some ways I always felt it might have been in a way less traumatic to lose a parent to death than to see everything I thought I knew and believed in end in divorce.

My wife Julie and I (having just celebrated twenty years of marriage) have had our ups and downs. We have also had some sharp exchanges and even our share of fights. However, in all of those exchanges, I don't remember one time when she or I ever considered divorce, separation, leaving the house. Neither of us ever threatened such a thing. Why? Because of my parent's example and the fact that her parents are fast approaching their fiftieth wedding anniversary. Both of us had good examples to follow and live by. Many times this is the edge that gets you through the tough times in a relationship.

The Unlikely Teacher

As ironic as it might seem, I got perhaps my best marital advice from a friend of mine who had been married and divorced three times. When I was fairly early in my marriage, I went through a period of time where I questioned my views on marriage—not just my marriage, but the institution of marriage in general.

I was at one of the impasses the marriage coaches warned of when we went through the required church-sponsored classes before exchanging wedding vows. They warned that most couples would experience periodic indecision and frustrations, warranting concern about the status of their relationship. This was one of those times of reflection in my life.

One day while having a drink after work I happened to express my concern to a good friend and business acquaintance of mine, Mark. As a man who had been divorced three times, he would surely have some insight to offer. He listened attentively and seemed very understanding.

After about ten minutes of listening to my concerns, he asked me to go out to his vehicle to listen to a new CD he had just gotten. This did not strike me as odd—he was somewhat of an audiophile and it was not uncommon for him to want to share his latest musical find.

However when we got into his vehicle, what happened next took me totally by surprise. Mark, a man who had been divorced multiple times, gave me some of the best marital advice I would ever receive.

"Larry, I want you to listen to me like you have never listened to anyone before. I am concerned where you are headed and it isn't good. You may think things will be better on the other side of the fence, but they aren't.

"All you will do your entire life is trade one set of problems for another, and you will never ever have the sanctity and purity of that first marriage. You can never get that back again. So unless you wake up one day and absolutely cannot stand the prospect of another day of marriage, fight for your relationship, and fight with everything you have.

"And for the record, if you talked to your wife about your concerns instead of me, your marriage would probably be much better off."

With that, it was over, we went back into the bar, finished our drinks, and he never said another word about it.

After much reflection that evening, I determined he was absolutely correct on all counts. I did start communicating with my wife about these and other issues, and it did make all the difference in the world. To this day I enjoy a very special and blessed relationship with my best friend and wife, thanks in part to this very unlikely mentor and coach.

As much as I would like to portray our marriage as living happily ever after, it's not that easy. Marriage is hard work, it is commitment, and it is sacrifice. Most if not all of these things don't seem to be in style with our present-day society, and that is a tragedy. We attempt to minimize the impact of divorce and its impact on society, but it is impossible to overestimate its true cost.

How to Pick a Winner

The biggest challenge for all of us is how to find that one person we can spend an entire lifetime with. This is not easy. Many are coming to the conclusion it is not even possible at all.

When my wife and I were first married, the professionals who taught classes in our church to prepare us for the sacrament told us that we would become drastically different people every seven years. In that respect, every seven years we would in fact decide whether or not to stay married. This has proven to be prophetic; what makes marriage challenging as well as hard work is making sure you grow together and not apart as you go through life.

The other and possibly more important challenge is making sure to look for the correct qualities in a life partner to begin with. One of the more interesting ways to train children and stack the deck in their favor was supplied to me by an elderly gentleman during a chance encounter at a business conference.

Date Nights

When my eldest child, Hillary, was about three years old, I had the fortune to go on a business trip in which I would learn a very valuable lesson. Not a business lesson, as one would expect on such a trip, but an extraordinary life lesson.

On this particular evening, the group I was meeting with was having a company-sponsored dinner at a posh restaurant in Chicago. I was seated next to a distinguished-looking gentleman from Kentucky. He was approximately sixty years old and was the principle owner of a complex of equipment stores. He was very successful and he looked it.

I was interested in conversing with him on a variety of business topics and trying to glean as much knowledge as possible in the short amount of time I would spend with him. However, before we got to the topic of business we talked of families. It soon became evident that no matter how successful he was in business, his first passion and proudest achievement was that of being a father. And what a brood he had, five of the most beautiful daughters you could ever lay eyes on, ranging in ages from twenty-five to forty years in age.

The more we talked about philosophies of raising a family, the less concerned I became of talking about business. As much as I wanted to know about his philosophies on the subject, I ascertained there was a more valued trove of information on the topic of families to be had. As we discussed our common philosophies on raising families, he asked me the most amazing question, in a rather pretentious tone.

"Larry, have you ever dated your daughter?"

"Excuse me," I said rather astonished by the question.

"Have you ever dated your daughter?" he asked again without batting an eye.

"No, not really...what exactly do you mean?" I asked, still reeling from the boldness and peculiarity of the question. Is it possible I could have misjudged this man? What on earth was this all about? I had never heard of such a thing! He then proceeded to explain what he was talking about.

"When my first daughter was about your girl's age, my wife and I sat down and talked about how we could instill in our children the values that we cherished. Additionally, we wanted them to respect themselves and other people and to never sell themselves short in life, especially...**especially** when it came time to picking the person they would spend the rest of their life with."

Intrigued, I asked him how they accomplished this and what this had to do with dating my daughter. They had obviously raised very sharp girls, who all seemed to have married extremely well. He had my undivided attention.

"Well", he said, "we decided the best way to do this was for me to take each girl out periodically on a special date night for dinner, and a movie or some other outing she wanted to do. On this night we acted as if we were on an official date. I called ahead to the restaurant and told them what we were doing, and they made it very special. We dressed nicely and I opened the doors of the car, restaurants, and other buildings for my daughter, just as a respectable date would do.

"My daughters, who would climb in the driver's side and into the back seat any other day of the week, would patiently wait by the passenger side door for me to come and open it for them. They would do the same thing at any exterior door of a building we happened upon."

Then came the ultimate punch line.

"And you know what Larry, when it came time for them to actually date...they would not settle for anything less," he said with a wink, obviously the plan all along.

"A young man came to the house one evening and honked his horn for my daughter to magically appear and run to the car. Not my daughter. She scoffed at this macho gesture, turned the outside light off, and calmly went up to her room and stayed there. Even when the young man finally came to the door, she didn't even acknowledge him. She knew better—this was not the way a gentleman behaved. My daughters soon got a reputation for these standards, and that young man was the last person who tried that."

The gentleman proceeded to tell me that he had a least one date every other month with each daughter until they reached their mid teens, and they still had their special nights every few months into their late teens. During these dates they talked about anything the girls wanted to discuss, hopes, dreams, and fears. That groundwork of communication served them well when the girls got into the difficult teenage and high school years.

Did I adopt this practice? You bet I did. Maybe not as religiously as he did but I averaged a date at least every few months. When my son came along, we adopted the same practice with a different twist; my son went on a date with his mother quite regularly from the time he was five. On those dates it was my son's responsibility to open doors for his mother and help her with her chair, starting early teaching him to be a little gentlemen. We also would periodically switch and do "boys' night out" and "girls' night out."

As my wife and I progressed down this path with our kids, we spread the word as more people noticed and asked about what we were doing. By the time my daughter was ten, it was not uncommon to see other fathers out with their daughters and mothers out with sons. And of course it would stand to reason that you would also have a date night with your spouse periodically as well. Needless to say, we were very proud that we helped spread those seeds and were able to see them grow in the community.

FAMILY MAKES THE DIFFERENCE

In conclusion, family support and guidance makes the difference as a person progresses through life, especially when we face the type of challenges described in this book. My immediate family was a big part of my recovery after the death of my mother, but also many extended relatives—aunts, uncles, and cousins—played a crucial role in this process. They helped show me the light when I could imagine nothing other than darkness.

Sadly, however, many of us do not have this backup because of decisions made by parents, many times out of expedience and selfishness. I know some may resent these comments as judgmental and simplistic. As noted before, I will take that risk.

For those who feel it is impossible to continue their marriage, please make the best of a bad situation by putting the children first. Make their welfare your top priority, not your own selfish needs for money, assets, and vengeance. Make their life as stable as possible, even if it means sacrificing some of your own goals and desires. Remember the promise that many of us made when looking into our children's eyes that first time, the promise to take care of them and put their interests ahead of ours no matter what…for the rest of our lives. **Lets all make good on that one promise, if we never keep another.**

Don't Leave it Unsaid

During the process of writing this book I had the opportunity to show an early draft of my transcript to my first cousin, Gary Schartz, one of my Uncle Junior's sons. I was intrigued and relieved by his enthusiasm about the book. During the course of our discussions, he told me of a letter his father had written to the family the day he was to undergo the exploratory surgery that would ultimately reveal his fate. Gary asked if I would like to see it; I was honored and excited that he would share such a personal thing with me to help further this project.

This extraordinary letter told of my Uncle Junior's very genuine love for his family and his regrets that he had not done a better job of outwardly expressing his love and affection throughout the years. As I read and reread the letter, I determined that this was another valuable lesson that my uncle was able to help teach us all. Don't leave it unsaid or at least unexpressed.

Many of us have trouble expressing our emotions and that is understandable. Depending on the culture and norms of a family, it may seem awkward to do so. However, it is important that we make the effort and continue to explore the many different ways to accomplish expressing what is inside each of us.

One obvious method, verbally communicating our feelings, sounds simple enough but many people cannot seem to do it. I will confess that within our family structure, it has not been common for the men in the family to say "I love you." To this day it is difficult for me to do this with my father. I hate it, but it is a fact. I do it more now than I did ten years ago, but not enough and it still feels a bit awkward.

I am changing that culture in my own family; we constantly express our love to our kids, and we don't plan to stop. I never want to develop that hesitation with my own children.

The next method is to express your feelings by writing them down and sharing them with your family. It may seem strange, but this method is a natural fit for me. I am somewhat famous in my family for my overly sentimental letters in which I detail just how I feel about family members. Even though I cannot verbally express these emotions at times, I have no problem writing them down.

The Last Line

This technique can be particularly helpful in the teen years. I recently heard a story of a particular parent whose lines of verbal communication were strained with her teenage daughter. During this period of time, she would slip written letters to her daughter by placing them under her pillow once a week. In the letters the mother would try to clarify her positions about certain items of contention in their relationship, and always emphasized that despite their current difficulties, her love was unconditional and she would be there when her daughter was ready to talk. These letters were never acknowledged by the daughter and rarely ever discussed between the two. They eventually got through these tough times and maintained their close bond together.

A few years later when they were moving the daughter's belongings to the university where she would soon be attending, the mother happened across a box in the closet. A neatly tied ribbon bound the box with a bow at the top. Curiosity got the better of her, and she asked her daughter about it. Upon her daughter opening the box, the mother was stunned to see all the letters that she had written her through the years, organized neatly within. The daughter tearfully admitted that she had read and saved each letter and that she would always treasure them. These letters very well could have been the last line of defense for their once very strained relationship.

Louder Than Words

Another way to express our emotions is by our actions. I have a sister-in-law whose family didn't verbally express their emotions. However, she does a wonderful job of demonstrating her love and emotions by all the special things she does for the people closest to her. If anything happens or a crisis emerges, if anyone needs anything, she is there. She is the first person to offer help in any number of ways. She demonstrates her love and caring by her actions; her compassion and emotions are unmistakable.

These are but a few examples. There are many other ways to demonstrate your emotions and love for those closest to you. Find the way that best suits your style and personality but— most importantly—do not wait.

CONCLUSION

This section of the book has dealt primarily with the question **why do we live?** More importantly...the importance of how we live and the impact our lives have on those around us.

How does this tie to the mission at hand? How we live impacts not only those important to us, it also impacts the **quality of our death** which then may well impact the lessons passed on and re-confirmed when we go through the process of dying. How at peace we are at the time of our death will have primarily to do with the quality of our relationships, friends, and most importantly our families.

The Kiss

I stole into his room that night, careful not to
make a sound.
I looked wistfully upon my child of nine, to gaze
with wonderment and pride, to reminisce
about another year gone by.

The accomplishments, the growth and yes even
the occasional disappointments.
The hugs, the spats, the pride and fury, all part of
a day, all part of a life.

The indescribable longing to suspend time, while
at the same time a breathless, impatient excitement to see what's next.
The understanding that life speeds by, barely a
blink, and that we are powerless except to
appreciate its wonder.

On this night, once again I serve my yearly tradition, the birthday kiss.
On this night, while in his peaceful slumber I
would kiss my nine-year-old boy goodbye.
Good bye to third grade, lunches at school, kisses
and hugs in front of friends, Cub Scouts, holding hands on walks, and yet another layer of
the sweet innocence of youth.

And in the morning, the start of a new day, I will hug
my ten-year-old hello. The joy of another school
year and new milestones to be reached, the won-
ders of growth, maturity and independence.

Yes, I will miss my nine year old as I progress through life.

From time to time I will reacquaint myself with those wondrous times, reminiscing through photos and my own recollections, even at times missing days gone by.

In the future, realizing that within that young man now in his twenties rests that nine-year-old child I loved so much.

Wrapped like wonderful layers, the very fabric of his existence, these layers always present, one atop another each adding to the whole, making us who we are.

It is our obligation not to lose those amazing children inside us all, children who appreciate the wonder of a starry night, splashing in a rain soaked street, and even laughing with little understanding of what we were laughing at.

Let us fight for those children, for the innocence that lies within us all.

Let us fight to recapture the magic of those childhood days.

So close your eyes on a rainy day and breath in the mystery of those special moments in time. It will come back to you, it surely will…

So when I kissed my nine-year-old goodbye that special night, I was not in reality saying goodbye.

I was acknowledging the wonder of God's greatest gift…children. Welcoming the wonder of growth, discovery, and the excitement of what lies ahead…our life's journey.

Lesson 5

The Fundamental Truths

"Insanity is doing the same thing over and over yet expecting a different result."

—Albert Einstein

"Good judgment comes from experience. And where does experience come from? Experience comes from bad judgment."

—Mark Twain

In this section of the book I will detail some key lessons learned over the past seventeen years since my uncle's death. His death brought about in my life much soul searching...no more than that—a search for the meaning of life and our very existence. What makes us tick? Why do we do what we do, and what drives us to go on? And more importantly, is it important that we go on? If so, why?

As I plunged headlong down this path of discovery, I have found some answers, but more importantly I have discovered what I refer to as fundamental truths. I define fundamental truths as those things that are accurate, will stand the test of time, and will help lay the foundations for a stable and productive life. Why is this important?

Because, if you are going to ever have hope of developing into a person others can follow and wish to emulate, if you are ever going to have hope of being able to finish well, you must know these fundamentals and live by them. They will act as the foundation of your life. If you understand and live by these truths, you will have a much better chance of maintaining stable and caring relationships with the people closest to you, be more likely to provide for your family financially, and have a better chance of being a role model worthy of followers. This will subsequently add up to being an emotionally stable person, a good friend, family member, and provider.

Finally, by following these fundamental truths you will be a person who will likely have the ability (and desire) to look past yourself and your own needs. To look at those around you and keep in mind their needs...yes even to the very end of your life. So please move ahead with me as we explore these fundamentals, the foundation of the Life Lessons.

At the end of the day, the world was either a better or worse place because you were on it. Because in the final analysis you gave more than you took.

The Fundamental Truths

As noted earlier, one of the most important things I've learned from my experiences over the past twenty years is that there are fundamentals, truths that will stand the test of time. Truths which will be as true one hundred years from now as they are currently. I have tried to define them, learn them, and implement them so that they are part of the bedrock of my life. One extraordinary example of this type of truth is what my Uncle Junior imparted to me on his deathbed that will be shared later in this story.

It should be noted that there are other fundamental truths and that I struggled with which ones to include in this book. I decided on these because I felt that they are germane to the subject at hand. For anything to qualify as a fundamental truth, it must meet the following criteria.
- It must be true,
- it must be relevant,
- it must be important, and
- it must be timeless.

The following are six of the fundamentals I have been able to identify and define at this stage of my life.

1. Own Your Emotions

Before I begin the discussion of owning your emotions it is important to answer a question that might emerge while reading this section. How does this topic differ from the forging of our emotions discussed earlier in the book? The section on the forging of our emotions deals primarily with how and why our emotions are developed, which differs greatly from owning and controlling our emotions once they are developed and a part of us.

While it is very important and possibly one of the most difficult things we will ever do, we must learn to own and control our emotions. Numerous people never master this art, they act impetuously out of convenience, vindictiveness, or naivety, saying and doing things that haunt them, many times for the rest of their lives. A number of people will never learn to control their emotions. Instead they will let their emotions control, sabotage, and rule their lives.

Owning and controlling emotions is especially important when we are dealing with death and tragedies. It is important to understand that we don't have to decide how we feel about certain issues, people, and events in the early stages, just after a tragedy occurs. Our perceptions are many times strained and even warped by the intense pressure and emotions we are dealing with at the time.

Recently, a friend of mine was dealing with a major setback in his life; he had lost someone extremely close to him. He and his wife felt pressured and even somewhat compelled to make decisions about the rest of their lives...as if it had to be done right then and there. How they felt about God, family relationships, and all the issues that surrounded the death—these had to be defined...almost immediately.

I told him that it was not necessary or even advisable to make important decisions too quickly. I further counseled him and his wife to sort out their feelings and emotions over a period of time. In situations such as this it may be important to let some of the raw emotions heal before making decisions that will impact your future and relationships with those closest to you.

2. LEARN TO NEGOTIATE

The term "negotiate" is generally understood as business terminology, a word that you would expect to see in a business text, not in a manual on how to live a good death. Fair enough. However, there are many types of negotiation. The traditional definition relates to negotiated issues such as wages, assets values etc., but included in our discussion will be important negotiated issues such as spiritual, balance of life, social, personal, family issues, and even physical concerns.

Negotiation is important to the quality and quantity of our lives. This is a general truth, one that will never be any less true. Negotiation is the key to success (all types of success) and survival. Our success at negotiating will almost always define much of who we are, how successful we are (in relation to how we **define success**), and ultimately even how happy we are. How well we negotiate in many ways defines and determines the quality of our lives. Therefore, it is important to understand the significance of negotiation and become trained (as well as possible) in the art and practice.

There are many books on the subject. Build your library and become a student, even an expert, on the topic, and learn to think win/win. Negotiation is not ultimately about wining and losing, it acknowledges the fact that the pie many times is big enough for both parties to win, to get much of what they want.

The Will and the Iceberg

Let me give you a brief example in relation to the issues at hand. Think about the division of assets and estate property after someone passes away. The classic reading of the will is many times where the ultimate breakdown of some families occur. Emotions are often volatile and there can be a lot at stake, so a breakdown is somewhat understandable. This makes it no less forgivable. Many family disputes occur over assets, many times rather insignificant (but meaningful) keepsakes. This is where being a good negotiator could save the day, or at least minimize the damage.

First, it is important to understand that what you see, the physical or displayed emotions, issues, or reactions concerning such an event are many times the proverbial tip of the ice berg. It wasn't the part of the iceberg that the crew of the Titanic saw that sunk the ship, it was in actuality what was beneath the surface that dealt the fatal wounds.

Therefore, all parties involved must not only take into account the assets, property, and special items, they must understand what is beneath the surface—the family pecking order, the middle child complexes, or whatever else prevails in the family political environment. It is these issues that will ultimately undo the negotiating process of any estate disbursement, as well as the fabric that holds a family together.

There are ways to deal with these potentially thorny issues. Negotiating a settlement in advance allows each family member to earmark a certain number of items as keepsakes, the rest to go into the estate to be auctioned off at a later point (additional items could be purchased at that time if family members wish). If more than one family member wants certain items, determine in advance how resolutions will be handled (drawing straws, flipping a coin, or something more scientific). If you define the process and rules of the process before it starts, disputes are less likely to arise or be irreparable.

The Other Half

Yes, we have the physical world. We need money to live, and resources such as food and housing to survive. And we will need to be good negotiators to help enable us to take care of our basic—and not so basic—needs. A number of books deal with those issues so in this book I will deal with what I call the other half.

Ultimately, what we will and should negotiate the most diligently for will likely be tied to our life's mission, what we hold dear, and what is truly important in our lives. In many cases this will not involve the pursuit of money and physical assets. Instead it will involve the pursuit of balance, living our spirituality, having an active and vibrant social experience, as well as taking care of our physical and intellectual pursuits in our life.

Just a few examples will demonstrate the difference. When my family had the opportunity to transfer to Salina from Great Bend for our company, it was an exciting opportunity on a lot of levels, offering a range of inducements for our family: religious education (through high school) for my kids; the opportunity for me to pursue teaching at the university level; and a broader social experience. While financially there was no incentive to move—the cost of living was higher in Salina for one thing—on balance, transferring brought a tremendous opportunity for my family and me to grow. Additionally it gave our company a much needed profitability gain by streamlining our business operations.

I recently went to a funeral of a man I considered a very good, even masterful, negotiator. He was also a man who died without ever having achieved great monetary wealth—he and his family led an average but comfortable middle class life. However, he made well-defined and well-thought-out tradeoffs his entire career so he could focus on those things important to him and his family. He turned down transfers (and the raises and the career opportunities that surely would have gone with them) to keep his children in the same community until they grew up and could make their own decisions. His family, his church, and service to his fellow man were the cornerstones of his existence. For most of his career he negotiated extra hours during the week so he could go on weekend trips with his family, and serve his church. I don't believe I have ever been to the funeral of a richer more prosperous man than this.

Three to Six

Finally, I must give as an example my own administrative accountant and secretary, Therese, a person who came into my life at just the right time to teach me an extremely valuable lesson.

When Therese came to work for our company she arrived with a sterling resume and glowing recommendations from previous employers (who I still hear from occasionally wanting to hire her back). She also arrived with an unquestioned work ethic and a balance in her life that was uncompromising.

Therese made it clear when she started work that two things were non-negotiable in terms of her employment. First, she would need to be done with work at three in the afternoon each day. Second, she would not work weekends and would need a week off each year to help direct a mission trip for the youth in her church. She made it very clear that she would get the job done whatever it was and would put in extra hours as needed to ensure that.

Out of curiosity I asked Therese why it was so important and such a necessity to be off of work by 3:00 each day. She said it was so she could be there when her then high school-age daughter and her middle school-age son got home from school. When I pressed her to expand her position, she pointed out that when her kids got home from school they were ready to talk. They talked about school, friends, boyfriends, girlfriends, almost anything she wanted to talk about...until about six in the evening when then they shut off, they move on...to homework, to the Internet, to their social network.

She went on to tell me that this was perhaps the most important time each day that she spent with her kids, and she was not giving that up for any job. Wow! Now that is a negotiator. Incidentally, I have learned the lesson and am practicing (as much as possible) the same approach with my own children...and she is absolutely correct. They sing like canaries during that three hour stretch on their way home from and shortly after school.

That's a Wrap

Hopefully, these three examples have illustrated that negotiation is about much more than money. It is about negotiating and standing for choices a person has made in relation to his or her life and mission. Negotiating is the act of defining what is important to you and fighting for it.

Will you always win? Certainly not. However you can't win a game or contest unless you know what you are fighting for, why it is important, and what you are will to do to attain your goals. By learning and employing good negotiating tools and techniques, hopefully you will get much of what you want in your life and pay only the price worth paying (whatever the currency may be).

3. Find Balance in Your Life

Many people at the time of their passing have deep-seated regrets about the balance they have chosen in their lives. While some of this is natural and will likely always be present, people must be aware of this so that the last days and weeks of life are not ruled by guilt over choices made and opportunities missed.

Therefore, it is important that as we live our lives we reflect on how we will feel about the priorities we have defined. Did we spend enough time with our families or did our careers and the pursuit of making money take over our lives? I am not insinuating that mothers should stay home or that parents cannot strive for success, I am simply pointing out that we should always do our best to keep it all (career, family, spiritual, and social) in balance.

Not Bad?!

Single mothers and even some couples are working two and three jobs to make ends meet, just for the necessities of life. Many times they have very few choices—they must put the hours in. And it is not my intent to make these people feel guilty or por- tray them as unfit or neglectful parents. They are not! They are doing whatever is necessary to provide the basic needs for their families and they should be admired and commended for that.

About five years ago I had a very interesting personal exam- ple of just how tough it is for a person to prioritize everything they would like. I was about forty years old and had decided as a sort of last hurrah to go out and play tennis at the highest competitive level for one last summer. My daughter was a third grader and my son fast approaching kindergarten and I knew that my tennis career (such as it was) would soon have to take a back seat to their lives.

As noted previously, I had played collegiate tennis and have through the years been a respectable competitive tennis player. Therefore I decided to play the open level (the highest level) events in the summer United States Tennis Association tourna- ments. I had a relatively successful season, winning over half my matches (playing mostly collegiate level players). My suc- cesses, coupled with my daughter Hillary accompanying me on all my trips, made it a very special summer for both of us.

During this time I played a tournament in my hometown. My sister Bev and my father came to watch me play. I did well in the tournament and even had the bonus of picking up a partner and placing well in the doubles bracket. That evening my sister described my father's reaction to the day's events. He was somewhat amazed at the level of tennis that I played. After reflecting momentarily, it suddenly became clear to me that this might well have been the first time he had seen me play. I had played in high school, college, and any number of other competitive tournaments but I don't think my father had ever had the opportunity to see me play competitively.

Why? Because he worked long hours, and it was not possible for him to take off during daytime hours when the tournaments took place. My father was not a neglectful parent, he just did not have the luxury of taking time off for events such as this. Other sporting events, such as high school wrestling, he rarely missed. Those were in the evening hours and did not involve taking leave of his daytime work responsibilities. My father and mother also took every vacation to follow my sister, brother, and myself when we were involved in drum & bugle corps as kids. It was just tennis he couldn't be part of.

In the era of kid-centered lives, many parents are made to feel guilty if they miss a game or in some cases even a practice. However, sometimes bringing home the bacon has to be our top priority. We must all strive to find the balance. It is not always easy, but it is always worth the effort.

Tools of the Trade

In the pursuit of doing the best we can to balance our spiritual, career, and family lives, many tools are available—planning systems that will help us to do just that. I believe the Franklin/Covey planning system is probably one of the best; it requires you (as part of its system) to plan all of your major roles in life (career, family, civic, spiritual, etc.). There are surely other systems. Find one that works for you and utilize it. Try to make sure that whatever issues you face at the time of your passing, regret and guilt are not among them.

Control your life and your time; do not let it control you.

4. Pick Your Battles Wisely

Before I start, yes another disclaimer so as not to oversimplify an issue. Some things are worth fighting over, for, and about, and some things are so unfair and repulsive that it is next to impossible not to hate another individual (think Osama Bin Laden, Hitler, Dennis Rader/BTK).

Some things are worth the price you pay (and yes, you do pay a price) to fight about. What is that price?

First and many times the inability to move on; until you let something go, it is impossible to put it behind you and move on with your life.

Second could be collateral damage to other relationships, people who through no fault of their own get caught up in the melee, the swirl of activity brewing around the fight. Take divorces and other family disputes for example. In most—if not all—cases, people are forced to take sides. Many times the process can insert a definitive wedge in a family.

Third, hate can and likely will eat you up, consume you from the inside out, and many times you will not realize it is happening until it is too late. You will have lost the person you were, in some cases having given up your very heart and soul to the rage you feel. Eventually, it will leave you as a shell of your former self. You will emanate a stench from your very pores that any normal, well-adjusted person will find incredibly offensive and even repulsive to be around.

Fourth is the opportunity cost in relation to your thoughts and deeds. While you are scheming, conniving, and fighting, there are many other productive things you will not have time to focus on and accomplish. Your mind will be so consumed with the battle, you might not recognize opportunities that present themselves during that same period of time.

The Water Molecule and the Brain Crane

Recently I had the good fortune to be sitting in front of the television, channel surfing different shows, when one in particular caught my attention. The show was called *What the Bleep do we Know?*

This show is a virtual think tank of ideas on the topics of the mind-body relationship as well as spirituality and how it all fits together. It is part fiction and part documentary, and is filled with the insights of many great thinkers, medical, philosophical, spiritual, and physical scientists.

I found two parts of the program particularly intriguing. One involved a photographic display in a subway station, a series of pictures of something not easily distinguishable. It turned out they were all pictures of water molecules from the same body of water. What made them intriguing was how differently each molecule was shaped. One looked like a square with a hole in it—the water after it was taken directly from the river. The next looked like a snowflake or a cross between a star and pentagon, with extremely intricate details—this molecule had been blessed by a religious leader. A third picture was different yet—another extremely intricate shape at least as wondrous as the last (but markedly different) from a bottle of water with the words "thank you" stuck to it. The final and most graphic molecule had a yellowish cast and was grotesquely shaped. It came from water in a bottle with the words "I hate you and want to kill you" on it.

The second part of the program involved a representation of the inner workings of the brain. It showed how tentacles on the surface of the brain actually connect with and fire in different areas that can potentially lead to different outcomes in one's life. It showed that people who exhibit a victim mentality tend to fire in different areas of the brain than those who feel in control of their lives. These connectors resemble cranes on a construction site, they go about their work tirelessly and non-judgmentally, following the instructions of the person whose brain they inhabit. The show went on to demonstrate that if a person changes his or her frame of reference and decides to take charge of his life, the crane eventually moves its base of operation to other areas of the brain that could and should lead to different, more positive outcomes.

The True Cost?

The human body is comprised of 80 percent water. According to the first example above, the composition and form of water is affected by any number of factors such as spirituality (the religious leader's blessing), a positive word (thank you), or possibly any number of other things.

Is it too much of a stretch to assume that a positive or negative slant in our lives—whether we have a victim mentality or feel we are in charge of our life and our destiny—would have an impact on the form of the water in our bodies? Would this then have an impact on which parts of our brain our signals are firing on? Maybe? Probably? I think it is quite possible.

Two lessons can be taken from this fundamental truth. First, if you have a positive outlook in life and feel you are in control of your destiny, good things will have a way of finding your doorstep. Is this guaranteed? Of course not...but it will hopefully give you pause and make you reflect even more about what the true cost of doing battle is. Second, negative signals, the consuming anger, the misuse of our time and resources, may all add up to a distorted perspective in our lives as well as numerous missed opportunities.

Think. Be careful and be vigilant about picking your battles. Make sure they are truly worth the fight.

5. We Don't Deal the Cards

Say it ten times to yourself rapidly, especially when your world seems to be coming apart through no fault of your own.

"We don't deal the cards."

So many negative things (and even positive in some cases) happen as a result of things we have little or no control over. Things like sickness, luck, death, terminal illness, inheritances, natural disasters, random acts of violence, and many others.

"We don't deal the cards."

Many times we just have to play the hand we are dealt—bad things often happen to good people. When we least expect it. And yes, unfairly so.

"We don't deal the cards."

"We don't deal the cards."

When the cards are not falling our way, we must try not to put too much pressure on ourselves. We must keep our determination and focus, and keep fighting for what we believe to be right and important. Many times we don't know where the light is at the end of the tunnel. We may never know but we have to keep trying and be ever mindful of the impact of our lives and on others.

Down...Set...

Perhaps the best analogy I can draw is that of the football running back who finds himself in the middle of a busted play (one that doesn't go as planned). Many of the greatest plays in professional and college football started as busted plays. The ball is handed to the running back and he heads toward a planned hole in the defensive line, but it is not there...not as expected. The opposing team has anticipated the play or some-one on the line has missed a blocking assignment. In instances such as these, running backs are drilled and indoctrinated with the same instructions: keep your cool, keep your legs churn-ing, keep spinning and moving sideways, and if you do all of this you might just get lucky enough to find another hole in the defense.

Life can be much the same way. Many times we hit the wall and we don't know where the hole is to the other side. But we must keep churning our legs and moving side to side—maybe we will find our opening and maybe we won't, but we must keep trying, keep moving, and keep fighting.

The life event involving the passing of my mother was the bust-ed play in my life...all I could see was an insurmountable wall and I had no idea how to get through, over, or around it. My family and new stepfamily (like diligent offensive linemen) helped provide the hole in the wall, the one that helped me break through...break through to a new life, a new me, and a new future.

In closing and most importantly, I believe if we can fully ac-cept that **we don't deal the cards**, it makes it easier for us to **accept what life has dealt us and move on**, get on with the rest of our life, and **allow ourselves to be happy once again**.

6. Don't Take Yourself too Seriously

Part of what makes our death so traumatic is that we take ourselves too seriously. We feel in some ways that the world and the people around us will not survive when we are gone. Indeed, most likely there will be some short-term adverse affects when we are gone—that is natural. However, if we have done a good job of pre-planning financially (i.e., life insurance), have done our best raising good and productive children, and kept our spouses abreast of what is going on financially and with general family life matters, they should all be fine without us...in the long term.

A fitting analogy: if you stick your hand in a bucket of water and leave it there for thirty minutes, when you take it out the water fills in like it was never there. No matter how important we think we are, that is somewhat how life is—it fills the gaps... it goes on without us. The pressure we feel in relation to what will happen to our loved ones after we are gone is understandable, but we shouldn't burden ourselves too much. People in most cases adapt to new circumstances no matter how unfortunate and traumatic.

It might further surprise us that some in our family may even flourish after our death. They will grow in ways not possible with us in the picture. This should not be viewed as a negative. These family members now have the opportunity (and freedom) to become themselves, not just your son or daughter. They will now try and experience new things they might never previously have been bold enough to attempt.

Don't take yourself too seriously. Laugh and laugh often. Hold on to the inner child inside. Learn to admit mistakes when you make them, apologize, move on, and try not to make the same one again. Don't try to put on an air of perfection—very few of us can live up to that and even fewer want the pressures associated with trying.

In closing, take yourself lightly, and your job and your family obligations seriously. The rest of it will likely take care of itself.

What's it all Mean and How's it Fit?

A good question and worthy of an answer. Much of this book deals with life's most challenging questions, i.e., why do we die, and why do bad things happen to good people?

The six fundamental truths are the foundational structure to answering the question **why do we live?** This chapter deals primarily with how we should consider living our lives and in many respects why it is important to live them at all. This section has dealt with the practicality of our lives (owning our emotions, learning to negotiate etc.), and these practical tools of life will eventually form the foundation for the quality of our lives, our relationships, and eventually our end of life issues. Therefore, I felt it important to deal with some of the technicalities of living when dealing with the issues of death and dying.

Lesson 6

Transition Points

"Ordinary men look for great events. Great men take ordinary events and make them great. Ordinary men wait for opportunities, great men seize them."

—Anonymous, Internet Circulation

What are transition points? Transition points are those events that thrust your life noticeably and sometimes uncontrollably in an altered direction. That direction can be either positive or negative. An example of a positive transition point could be the birth of a child; an example of a negative transition point, the death of a parent.

Transition points exist, the only question is how intense they are and whether they are a positive or a negative force in our lives. Interestingly enough, the same type of event may be positive for one person and negative for another depending on the circumstances. Take for example the birth of a child. How that is viewed depends on different circumstances and conditions:

- Planned or unplanned
- Married or unmarried
- Income level
- Number of previous children
- Stability of the marriage
- Maturity level of the parents
- Age of parents (too young or too old)

All of us in a normal state of mind would find it difficult to view the birth of a child as anything but positive, but this is not always the case. Children are abandoned, aborted, or at the very least put up for adoption because pregnancies are unplanned and unwanted.

Ironically, the same case could be made in relation to the death of a parent. If a parent dies, one that has always been mature and loving as well as a good family leader, it will no doubt be viewed as an extremely traumatic and negative transition point. On the other hand, if the parent has been abusive, neglectful, and an extreme burden on their children, it could actually prove to be a positive transition point.

In some cases, even children who have had a very positive relationship with their parents may find that over time, the death of a parent has moved their life positively forward. This would be no fault of the parent and should not be viewed necessarily as a bad thing. Many times people will grow substantially after a parent's death, finding and defining their own identities, growing in ways not possible before. This can be a natural and positive process. Inarguably, in most cases the initial effect will be negative but eventually it may well move their life in positive directions.

In essence what determines whether an event is positive or negative is not in many cases the event itself or its immediate impact; it is the overall effect the event has on your life **over time**. Therein lies the complicated nature of transition points.

FIRST UNDERSTAND THAT THEY EXIST

First and foremost, it is crucial that people understand the concept of transition points and that they exist. Second, it is equally important to grasp the impact these events can have on our lives. And finally, understand that we can in many cases manage and even control that impact. Managing and controlling the impact is not easily done, but it can be accomplished.

The following are some examples of transition points that commonly occur in most people's lives.
- Births
- Deaths
- Weddings
- Graduations

- Kids moving out of the house (for the first time)
- Kids starting school (kindergarten)
- Education attainment
- Divorce
- Job status changes
- Legal troubles
- Health issues
- Geographic changes (moving to another city, state or location within a city)
- Money
- Boomerang kids (those that leave and then come back)

This is not meant to be an all-inclusive list; there are certainly many more.

Identify Them and Map Their Expected Impact

The most important thing about transition points has been discussed—acknowledging that they exist and are a factor in our lives. After we have acknowledged them, what then? Next, I suggest developing what I refer to as a transition map, the process of actually identifying the future and past transition points in your life.

Yes, I suggest even looking at the past transition points. Review what they were and how you handled them. With hindsight as your guide, think about what changes you would have made if you had it to do over. By doing this, you should get a good feel for how you can map and plan for future events in your life.

After you have reviewed the past, map likely future events in your life—birth, college educations, weddings, and yes, even deaths. How will you face these issues, both the good and the bad? Think about what your emotional state will be at that time, as well as the state of your family. Think about how you will manage your own mental and emotional wellbeing and how you can help lead others through the same experiences. Think about how you want to feel after the event is past. Visualize it, experience it, and most importantly plan it.

There are two types of transition points that we will all experience throughout our lives...planned and unplanned.

Planned Transition Points

Planned transition points are those events you know are going to happen and have some idea when. Events such as graduations and weddings would normally be good examples of these types of points. However, it is possible that the same type of event could be either a planned or unplanned transition point. Take for instance a wedding. It could be planned or it could be unplanned (if the couple eloped). The same could be said of a death—a person could die of a prolonged terminal illness or could be taken by a sudden event, such as a heart attack.

Unplanned Transition Points

It is many times the unplanned transition points (those that are unexpected and often traumatic) that cause the most upheaval in our lives. The sudden death of a loved one, or a spouse filling for divorce with little or no warning are examples of those events that could rock our worlds and often send our lives into a downward spiral. Am I suggesting there is an easy answer for this type of event? No, certainly not. We can however take a cue from the business world and do what is referred to as contingency planning.

How to Plan for Them

How do you plan for transition points in your life, the positive and negative, the planned and unplanned? Surprisingly there are many innovative ways to do this. I will visit a few of them in this section of the book. First, we will look at examples of planned transition points and how we can manage those.

It seems weird to think that we would need to go through this process for something that is both planned and positive, but keep in mind that sometimes these can really take us out if we are not careful. Let's take a combination of the empty nest syndrome and the weddings of our children. Many of us will lose all of our children to college and/or marriage in the span of ten years. I think we would all agree that these are in most cases planned and positive events in the short-term. But what must we be cautious of? What must we manage? **The long-term effect as much as the short-term.**

Many long and seemingly happy marriages end during this stage of life. Why? Because people did not look down the road and see potential problems coming. They did not realize that a positive event could actually have negative ramifications. Many married couples become so engrossed in their children's lives that they loose touch with the image of themselves as a couple. They are so busy taking part in activities, rushing to games and practices, that they have lost touch with each other and their marriage.

What to do…? Reconnect!

Reconnect with that which brought you together in the first place, **B.K.** (before kids). Rediscover each other and do it before the kids are gone. I would suggest this process begin in the early stages of your kid's high school careers. Have date nights, take a weekend getaway alone, and redefine and reestablish your social network that might have long been neglected. Take part in a marriage encounter group that includes a weekend getaway.

Possibly consider relocating, maybe not out of the city or the state but across town. I know one couple who had always had their eye on a certain house. It became available and they purchased it! He told me, "It was really neat, it knocked us out of a funk, gave us an exciting forward look at our lives instead of reflecting back on our past."

Do we forget our children? Certainly not, we still nurture them and support them. We simply redefine our own lives, so that our existence does not have to revolve around them anymore. Believe me, your young adult kids will appreciate it in the long run. Some other ways that you can find a new passion in your life in relation to planned transition points:

- Find a new hobby.
- Buy a new car
- New clothing and new look.
- Travel
- Join the country club and take up golf or tennis.

One nice thing about transition points such as graduations and weddings is they may free up income that for years has been tied up (i.e., saving for college and weddings). One couple I know even bought a second home at a favorite vacation spot. Remember, it might be best not to spend it all (think of those boomerang kids and the needs of aging parents), but have some fun with at least part of the new windfall.

PLANNING THE UNPLANNED

Next let's discuss how we can plan the unplanned. Those unexpected life events such as untimely death or divorce. I will take these two as examples because I think most of us would agree that they can be two of the most traumatic negative transition points.

First, let us revisit what I referred to a short while ago, the concept of <u>contingency planning</u>. Contingency planning is normally used in the context of business planning but I think it lends itself extremely well to this topic. Contingency planning is looking at the "what ifs" in our lives. What if I, as a husband and provider, live a good long life? What if I die in my mid-thirties? Each of these scenarios involves a different plan and since we don't know which will occur, many times we have to plan for the worst-case scenario.

So what types of things can we do to plan for the worst in relation to these types of transition points? There are quite a few things actually. First and foremost, we can make sure we are insured properly so that our family's future will be secured in the event of our untimely death. This would include providing ten times (recommended by the insurance industry) our annual income level in base insurance, mortgage insurance to pay off the mortgage, and even prepaid funeral expenses. In our twenties, thirties, and forties, insurance is very inexpensive (especially term insurance) and readily available to couples wanting to achieve the ultimate contingency plan.

Secondly, we can make sure our spouses understand our finances and even talk about and define a plan of action for them to follow if we should pass away (make sure they know what you have and where it is). And finally, make sure that wives as well as husbands establish their own credit. If she is a homemaker, put part of the credit you attain for your family in your wife's name.

In the case of an unexpected divorce, a wife in particular has a few options that could help secure her life. First, she can have her own career. Many of the most vulnerable women are those who have made the sacrifice of giving up a career early in their marriage. I know this is controversial and many women want to be stay at home moms, and I am certainly not against this. But if you have a career before marriage, keep at least one foot in the door. That will make it easier to kick-start your career again if necessary in the future. As in the case of premature death of a spouse, it is beneficial for a wife to establish her own credit separate from her husband. My wife has her own credit rating and even has a little better credit score than me. I do not feel threatened by this, and I readily encourage it.

With the odds of staying married at approximately 50 percent, I think it is ill-advised not to make contingency plans for divorce. We all hope it is not necessary, but who can be sure. Enjoy the best and plan for the worst.

FINAL THOUGHTS

Recently my father had open-heart surgery, a triple bypass, to repair a major defect in his heart. The surgery was to take place in Kansas City. During my drive to Kansas City from Salina, to be with him the next day, I had time to reflect on the different outcomes that could happen.

First and most likely, the surgery would be successful and my seventy-three-year-old father would have many more years of life to enjoy with his family. Second, the surgery would be unsuccessful and result in his death. Third and finally, it would be a failure, not resulting in his death but in a somewhat debilitated existence for him from that point on. While the final two possibilities were highly unlikely—and the third the most unlikely—I considered each one on the drive down.

What types of issues would I face with each and how would I react? Going through these scenarios in your mind may not be pleasant, but it can be beneficial. It is like any situation in life—the likelihood of getting through any challenging event increases proportionally to the planning and preparation you have done in advance.

If my father had died from the surgery, no doubt it would have been a huge setback in my life. What it would not have done is set me on my ass. I had thought about the "what if" scenarios and had a plan for each, and this gave me a sense of empowerment and peace of mind. I know my father would have wanted just that, and he has told me so on many occasions. As one of the leaders in my family, I would not have had the luxury of melting down. People would have looked to me for leadership and guidance. Due to my preplanning I would have been in a position to provide that, just as I have seen my father do on numerous occasions in the past when a family crisis hit.

And yes...plan to cry. There is certainly nothing wrong with that—it is the healthy product of a lifelong bond.

Part Three

Autumn Corridors—Death, the Final Lesson...

Autumn corridors fill our lives with dream homes; vacation homes, management, partnerships, factory floors, hospitals, and the many failed and fulfilled dreams. These corridors often times lead to disillusionment and a readjusting of our priorities.

Corridors that introduce us to the reality that there is no magic, that we are impotent and powerless in the face of death, destiny, and the many other forces that impact our lives.

Chapter 1

The Bad Death

There are bad, painful, traumatic, tortuous deaths. That is a fact. Deaths occur in which finding any meaning or redemption is nearly impossible. I feel it is important that I acknowledge this, otherwise, it would be far too easy to discount this work.

An increasingly common way to die as our society enjoys the fruits of longer lives is that of succumbing to the disease of Alzheimer's. Fortunately my family has not experienced this firsthand. I cannot imagine a more devastating experience for a family to go through, an extended, usually grueling progression of watching a person they know and love decline and become increasingly erratic as death approaches. For many, a death such as this might be very difficult to probe and find the silver lining within.

GOD IN THE ROOM?

As I was in the early stages of writing this book, an event in Kansas shocked not only the state but also the entire nation—the arrest of a confessed serial killer. As I watched the coverage with the rest of the nation, interviews were conducted with family members of some of the victims. I remember a common thread through those interviews: lives were destroyed and, though some of the murders had taken place as many as thirty years before, many of the victims' families never fully recovered from those devastating events.

One family member recalled the painful day when he and his sister (both still children at the time) discovered their murdered family, and told of the horror of the murder scene. In a harsh and cold tone he said that he looked around the room that day and did not see God in that house. Bitterly, he wondered where God had been that day and how He could have allowed this horror to happen to his family. Who among us would not feel similar feelings of betrayal, at least initially, and possibly for the rest of our lives.

As I watched this and similar stories in this horror-filled drama unfold, I wondered what good this book could bring to people who had suffered as much as they had. Is there anything that anyone could say, comfort that anyone could offer, to possibly restore a person's faith when it has been this badly damaged? I think that while there might be someone who could say something to help, the capture and bringing to justice of the killer will likely do more to bring closure for these people than anything any of us can do or say.

Therefore I will not attempt to offer some canned or expedient words of wisdom, or profound thoughts. What I will attempt to do is offer some possible explanations as to how tragedies such as these might actually be necessary to fulfill God's ultimate design.

But the ultimate question remains; how could an all-knowing, all-loving God allow something like this to happen to so many good people?

GOD'S DESIGN

Some people take the bible literally and believe that God controls everything that happens here on earth. Some even believe that everything happens for a reason, and everything is predestined.

Others believe that God gave us the Earth and all its vast resources, put the key components of life into motion, gave us his only son to show the path…and then got out of the way. We are then able to exercise free will and do as we will with everything He has blessed us with.

While I am not a biblical expert by any stretch of the imagination, I tend to concur with the second theory. I believe God has given us what we need to make life work, but we, exercising free will, do with it as we will. We, the human race, can do wondrous things with our lives and what we have been given. We can also do horrific things to the planet, civilizations, and each other if that is our wish. I do not believe for a moment that God moved this serial killer to take the lives of these innocent people or that it was somehow predestined to happen. I do not believe this any more than I believe the devil influenced him to do it. I believe he made the decisions to do what he did on his own. Evidence has already shown that he was very calculated and had dreadfully defined reasons for committing all of those horrific acts.

Consider the inverse of these tragic situations. Any time there is a plane crash or a natural disaster people are quoted as saying that God saved them from harm or death. If this is true, what made the others who perished less worthy of God's intervention than these particular people? I do not believe one deserved saving any more than the other. The laws of probability are in play, not necessarily the predestined intervention of God.

I believe victims of deranged and evil individuals such as the one illustrated above are unfortunately in the wrong place at the wrong time. It is tragic that in that place, at that time, they caught the attention of such an evil, heartless, and calculating person.

In the same vein, I believe that natural disasters are equally indiscriminant. The December 2004 tsunami that hit Indonesia was a tragedy on a global scale, but I don't believe for an instant that it was the wrath of God, or God's design to kill so many innocent people. This was a coastal region by an ocean with a history of underground movements. Tsunamis like this have probably happened periodically throughout history and will likely happen again. It is a tragedy, no doubt, but it is a natural disaster, not an act of God.

I do not mean to imply that it is never useful to ask for God's intercession—many well-documented examples of miracles exist in our human history. I simply do not believe it happens on a regular basis. It is not part of the natural order.

On the other hand, if God's design involves us having to experience a full range of emotions during our life here on earth, which I believe it does, there is only one way for this to happen. We must experience the full range of emotions firsthand, from the very good to the very bad. As noted earlier in the book, I believe this is why bad things happen to good people, why tragedies occur, and why the good die young. These, in part, are the very events that stimulate and develop emotions throughout our lives.

FREE WILL

One thing that most people of faith agree upon is that one of the basic tenants of nearly all doctrines involves the exercise of free will. If we believe in the concept of free will, then the serial killer discussed above had the free will to do the horrible acts he committed just as he had the free will to have refrained from them. Neither God nor the devil made him commit those murders, he made those choices deliberately and with intent. By way of his personal chilling confessions, it was very obvious he was very much in control of his own will at the time of these horrific crimes.

ETERNITY AND HEAVEN

If we believe in heaven, then is living another day here on earth to be viewed as a reward? If a person has lived a worthy life and is destined for heaven, the shortest time spent on earth could be argued to be the best-case scenario. Additionally, if we think about the concept of the vastness of eternity in relation to earthly pain, whether it is emotional or physical, unpleasant things that happen to us on Earth are largely irrelevant. Viewed in relation to eternity, the entirety of our existence here on Earth is far less than the blink of an eye and is just as irrelevant if heaven and eternity wait as our reward.

This is not meant to diminish the pain we all experience, but it might help to at least put it into a much larger perspective, helping us to appreciate why God might be tolerant and even accepting of our suffering (to achieve the larger goal of helping us to become divine).

Unfortunately, everything that works for us in life—our survival instinct, our physical protection mechanisms, and our insatiable will to live—ultimately works against us in the process of our death. Those same tools that so diligently protect us in life tend to make our dying process a painful, messy, and unpleasant experience.

YOU WERE SAYING?

I struggled with the idea of even including this section in this book. I am not sure what I hope to accomplish but I feel the need to acknowledge those deaths that will provide little or no meaning. There will be no redemption or reconciliation, there will be no closure, and there may be only pain, sorrow, and despair. The only solace for those deaths is time. Time is the ultimate resolution, the only relief in some cases. However, I do feel that in the majority of instances this is not the case…which is why I write this book.

Chapter 2

Life in Retrospect — How to Finish Well

I stirred for a moment and awoke to the sound of two dogs playing in the grass next to me. I was aware of their presence, nonetheless, I could not fully wake...my eyelids simply would not stay open.

When I awoke later, I was not sure how much time had passed. This time, however, my eyes could open, and my eyelids felt much lighter. As I lay in the grass I heard the sound of my heart beating—not only audible, it was beating quite rapidly. I was in a place I knew...knew very well, I was just unsure how I got there.

I was lying under a cluster of large oak trees in the Ellinwood City band shell park across from the majestic turn-of-the-century limestone Catholic church, of this there could be no doubt. I knew this place well. There were about a dozen or so people in the park though none seemed aware of my presence. The only creatures that seemed aware of me were the dogs I had heard playing earlier. I am not sure how much time had elapsed, but evidently it was enough to have used the dogs' excess energy because they both rested nearby, content to lie passively and gaze curiously at my face. Why the dogs showed such interest, while everyone else in the park was indifferent to me was unclear.

The dogs were very undistinguished, toy poo-dle sized with various shades of browns, grays, and blacks in their coat. I had a few sets of dogs like this as a boy, always mutts I had gotten for free from a friend or acquired quite reasonably from the dog pound. There was no money in the budget for pure-bred dogs, not in those days. These two, their size, their color reminded me in a way of...

Suddenly the two dogs sprang to their fours and proceeded together about twenty feet from where I was positioned, turned and gazed at me again, this time apparently waiting on something...was it me?

I ignored them, still trying to ascertain why I was here and what was next. I got up and started to walk toward a small group of people assembled a short distance away. As I walked toward the group, I became aware of a strange sensation, a distinct feel-ing that I was being watched. I turned suddenly and found the eyes belonged to one of the two dogs. The other dog was faced away from me; the one looking at me now was obviously the dominant of the two.

As our gazes met, the lead dog suddenly turned and trotted away from me. It seemed evident that I was to follow, which I did. I was not sure why but for some strange reason I felt compelled to do so.

As I walked the streets I knew so well, my new acquaintances and I passed by many stately early 1900-era houses. The sun was shining and the street was well shaded by the mature oaks and elm trees. The richness of the grass and the fullness of the trees gave me the impression it was mid-summer, but it should have been much hotter than this, if it actually was deep summer in Kansas.

As I examined the large and distinguished houses along the street, many of which I had admired my whole life, something struck me as odd. The houses...they looked normal enough...it was the windows; there was glass there, but I was unable to see through them. I tried very hard to catch a glimpse of anything on the other side of the windows, a piece of furniture, a lamp, movement of a person within, it was simply not possible.

Suddenly, my concern for this minor amusement disappeared as we rounded the corner of Bismark Street. At this point Ellinwood High School came into full view to my immediate left (the distinguished early 1900s railway station lay a couple of blocks straight ahead). The school was a very large and remarkable looking building, a dark brown brick structure as imposing as it was remarkable. This was the very high school that most of the members of the Schartz family had gone to for generations. It had a beautiful lawn and a wonderful stand of billowy oaks dotted all over the front and side lawns, providing a solid canopy of shade.

It was here that through the years I felt a spiritual connection with my mother. I imagined that this place had been witness to some really wonderful times for her. Any time I was in Ellinwood I walked or drove by... it felt as if I could almost...

Suddenly, I became aware that the time of day appeared to have changed, almost within a moment of time. Earlier it had seemed sunny and the sun was positioned straight up in the sky. Now it felt more like dusk and I could not locate the sun at all.

That is when it happened...every window in the high school, well over fifty of them, lit up instantaneously. This even startled the two dogs still slightly ahead of me. Was it getting darker? The lights sprang dramatically from the windows as if it were a pitch-black night with no moon.

About this time the dogs both looked back, after a last curious glance, both began running away from me. We were on the side of the high school and they ran toward the front of the building, moving quickly as though their owner had suddenly called for them. I saw them round the corner toward the front of the building, which is when I lost sight of them. Neither dog was the least concerned about my whereabouts now. Evidently, their job was done...or so I thought.

I quickened my pace to see what the dogs might have found so interesting. There they were, both sitting patiently looking up at the front door of the high school building. I moved toward the sidewalk that fronted the school toward the street and walked along the pavement looking guardedly up toward the building that still looked like a beacon in a dark landscape. As was the case before, I was not able to see what was on the other side of the windows, the light pushed mercilessly out while at the same time not letting anything back in.

That was it...everything from these windows, whether in the schools or the homes, everything pushed out, nothing could penetrate in. Not even the sun, which would have at least provided reflections.

I was directly in front of the building now. The dogs still sat patiently looking up at the front door, oblivious to my presence some thirty feet behind them. I was now standing on the sidewalk that led to the main entryway of the building, the place now occupied by my new little friends. I waited...but for what...and for how long?

After a few minutes that seemed much longer, I noticed a change in the light at the front doors, a slight flicker to begin with. That is when I saw the two shadowy images begin to gradually emerge from the light behind the windowed doors. At first very vague, as they came closer to the door the shapes began to materialize and became a bit clearer. Still it was impossible to make out what they were.

Then the doors opened...

The Good Death?

M any manuals and countless how-to books tell us how to live our lives. However, very few teach us how to die. In this section of the book I will not attempt to teach people how to die—dying is a unique and personal act that is not and should not be defined. Yet, I will give some suggestions and ideas on how the process of a forewarned, preplanned death might and could take place.

Before we begin, however, I want to make it perfectly clear what I am not attempting to do. I am not attempting to cast judgment or put undue pressure or expectation on another person's physical death (or even my own for that matter). I am not implying that everyone should magically mask their physical pain or that people will not or should not take anguish at their own passing. Just as people go through natural stages of grief in relation to other people's deaths, those same or similar stages occur in relation to one's own death. Fear, anger, panic, and various degrees of pain are all natural to feel, and to portray this as bad or somehow as a sign of weakness would be a terrible disservice for this project. It is as natural to experience the emotions and fear associated with your own death as it is to experience grief with the passing of others.

There is nothing wrong with being afraid to die. But as with any challenge we face, being able to manage and even conquer that fear could ultimately define and enhance our legacy. So consider this section of the book as an outline or checklist of things to consider as we all eventually go through the dying process.

How to Finish Well

It is somewhat ironic that our bodies likely possess DNA signals that instruct us to die well. However, in this day and age of instant gratification, "it's all about me" and "what have you done for me lately," I suspect many people would not recognize these signals when they arrive. It is probable that we would send them directly to our mental junk mail box.

Ronald Wilson Regan once said to Jimmy Carter in a famed presidential debate, "There you go again." Well, here I go again. I have already told you that you do not totally own your death. Now I will tell you that you do not totally own your life, either. Yes you can technically do most anything you want, but if you have lived a good and fruitful life, many people have a vested interest in you and what happens to you. They are like stockholders in a corporation—not the corporation itself, but stakeholders. What happens with and to you directly (or indirectly) affects their lives and their well-being. Therefore, how you finish your life will likely be very important to those that have been an active part of your life.

The Best Days

Before we talk more about how to finish well, let us look at a cold hard fact that must be dealt with directly in relation to our lives. For most of us there will come a day when we have to acknowledge that probably the best part of our life is behind us. The following words come from my father:

"Larry, you will spend most of your life looking to the future, because you have a future. However, there will probably be a point where your future is short and bleak due to a terminal illness. At that point in your life, you take solace by looking back, taking stock in your life, reflecting on all the good you have done and what you have been able to accomplish with God's greatest gift…your life.

"If you have led a good life, this review should provide great comfort, pride, and even much joy. If you have not, it could be a bleak and depressing time."

Some might feel—maybe after the death of a spouse later in life—that they are already at the point of taking stock. However, God may show them the way toward another spouse who can help fulfill their later years. Many of us will not find that second act—time or circumstances will not permit it. So, as my dad noted, we will and should look back on all the blessings we have been presented with.

But we can also do one more very important thing. We can find a way to give a little more in return on the way out the door. Find a way to give to others in need, remembering those that helped us when they could have simply faded away. Several ways to do this follow.

- Fulfilling your life through service to others
- Meals on wheels, working with homeless, teaching basic life skills
- Assisting as a volunteer with youth in schools
- Retired executive program
- Teach
- Run for public office
- Help as a volunteer with the local Chamber of Commerce
- Be a friend to someone in a nursing home
- Help others that are in need financially
- Work part time to stay active and plugged into life

There are many ways to stay integrated in the community and give something back. The important thing is to give life one last chance, keep fighting and leave it all on the court (a good basketball analogy). Most importantly, when you die you should be ready for the rest.

Frank and Ada

At this time I would like to highlight two people in my family who have done an exceptional job of showing others how to finish well—my Great Uncle Frank and his wife Ada.

Frank, who retired at sixty-five from the body shop business, took up carving after retiring. He had natural talent and did some wonderful work in his later years. I asked him once how he created a particular piece, a really wonderful carving of an Indian, and he said, "Larry, you start with a block of wood and simply carve away everything that doesn't look like an Indian"

My Uncle Frank did an amazing thing in the last weeks of his life that astonished me as well as others. Knowing how difficult it would be for Ada after his death, and unknown to anyone at the time, he made tapes for his beloved wife. When she was feeling sad and lonely, his voice on those tapes reminded her that he was still with her, that his love would live on forever, and that he would patiently wait for her to join him in Heaven.

My Aunt Ada, who just celebrated her ninety-second birthday is just as amazing. At ninety-two she still lives independently in her own house, does her own shopping, and even mows her own lawn. She has an indomitable spirit that will not be conquered, and she will live and fight until her last breath. On a rare occasion, she did question the good of living as long as she had, asking "Larry, what good can come of it? You just begin to feel like a burden." I was amazed that she would question the value of her life and I replied, "Ada you are showing all the people you love and care about how to be ninety-two years old and you are doing so quite gracefully." No college course teaches us how to age gracefully and live a full and complete life, we learn it primarily by example, watching those closest to us. What a wonderful example my Uncle Frank and Aunt Ada have been in my life…we just sit back, watch, and take notes…and yes, we are watching.

THOSE WHO FINISHED WELL

As I was initially putting this project together, I knew this section would be part of the book. As I started to write the opening sections, I began to think about compiling a short list of those who had finished well. People who fought back the fear and trepidation, sucked it up, and ran hard and fast to the finish line. Over the course of a year I came up with an extensive list of people who fit that category. I will list and highlight a few that I feel are shining examples in the art of finishing well.

Salute

Without a doubt the best example of finishing well are those who have died in the defense of our country. Many of these fought to their last breath while defending our country, liberty, and freedom. A great example is the invasion of Normandy in World War II, particularly during the landings at the beach. It is astonishing that those men could muster the courage to leave those boats. They knew the odds, they knew a number of them faced certain death and would not make it to the other side of that beach alive, but they did what they had to do. All of them, I am sure, were terrified, but they conquered that fear in the face of the most challenging of circumstances. Throughout this book, I give honor to the military men, women, and their families for their courage, service, and sacrifice.

Jesus Christ

Jesus by his death gave us life and the hope of salvation. He was teaching and prophesizing to his last breath, and with his final act he gave us the chance for salvation and an eternity in heaven.

Spencer Tracy

One of my favorite movies of all time is *Guess Who's Coming to Dinner* starring Katharine Hepburn, Spencer Tracy, and Sidney Poitier. While this is obviously a wonderful movie in its own right, garnering ten academy award nominations and winning two of them, what was wonderful about this movie was the real life drama behind the actual production of the film.

What many people do not realize is that Spencer Tracy was suffering from a terminal illness at the time the movie was filmed. He was in fact ailing so badly that Columbia Pictures was balking at making the film with him, and insurance companies were refusing to insure the project. Stanley Kramer and Katharine Hepburn wanted Tracy so desperately for the project that they did the unthinkable—they agreed to put their salaries in escrow to secure the project. The following quotes are from the filmmaker, Stanley Kramer:

"We (Kramer and Hepburn) agreed not to take a penny, so that if anything should happen to Tracy, our combined moneys could be used to make the film with another actor."

They utilized reduced filming schedules to help preserve Tracy's energy. Kramer notes:

"He had no physical energy for the shooting of this film, and so we had to film it only in the morning. Columbia didn't know we shot only half days. Well of course we did finish the picture... and ten days later he (Spencer Tracy) was dead."

What a wonderful story, picture, and real life example of how to finish well. On your next visit to the video store, rent or buy this extraordinary movie and watch it with new eyes for the miracle and truly inspirational story that it is.

Christopher Reeve

Hollywood recently lost a talented and inspirational figure in Christopher Reeve. Seriously injured in a horseback riding accident many years ago, this one-time leading man could have easily retreated and withdrawn from life. Instead, he utilized his celebrity status and considerable influence to help further spinal cord research. He also did some additional acting and maintained an extensive travel and public appearance schedule through the later stages of his life.

Pope John Paul II

The world lost one of its most dynamic and charismatic religious leaders of all time recently with the passing of Pope John Paul II. In the twenty years of his papacy, he was dynamic and energetic until Parkinson's disease took hold of his increasingly frail body. He fought a long and determined battle against the disease, finally succumbing to its ravages in May of 2005. The disease never conquered the physically weakened pope's spirit however. He maintained much of his public schedule until the final weeks of his life and exhibited his truly indomitable spirit until the very end. He was truly a pope and a human being who showed us firsthand how to live well and how to die well.

And Finally

People will watch how you live your last days, and you will be teaching as you proceed down that path. Furthermore you will be delivering messages to your friends and loved ones by your words and actions in those final days, weeks, and months. What will they be?

Let's think for a moment about the messages we spend our lives teaching our children. Two of the most important are finish what you start, and never give up.

How you live your final days could very well undo a life's work by sending your friends and family conflicting messages. Do not deny your physical pain or emotions, but by your words and actions send the clear message that all life matters. All the stages of your life can positively impact others.

I will end this section of the book with a story about Max, a very dear friend of mine who recently lost his wife after forty-nine years of marriage. Both were fast approaching retirement age and had been planning to begin their formal retirement in the very near future. Then one evening without notice, the love of Max's life was struck down with a very swift blow.

I had lunch with him a few weeks after her death. He was asking many of the questions that come up after such a thing happens. Why didn't the Lord take us at the same time? What will life be like without her? How will I find the strength to go on?

I was working on this book at the time, this chapter in particular, and I was able to offer at least partial answers to these questions. Did they totally ring true that particular day? Probably not. He is still in a fog, as though he has been through traumatic surgery and is still coming out from under the anesthesia. He may not even totally remember the answers. In a couple of months I will have him to the house for dinner and another visit, reiterating the themes of my previous conversation.

At least now I am not struck by silence. I do not avoid a person like Max because I have no idea what to say, what to think, what to do. I hope this book gives people a way to be an active part of the healing process when those closest to you are dealing with the loss of a loved one.

Chapter 3

The Planned/Expected Death

Then the doors opened...

The two women who emerged through the doors were two of the most beautiful women I have ever seen. One I recognized from somewhere, I didn't know where. She wore a tight dress and a 1920s style hat that, along with her sleek sexy shoes, made her look extremely exotic.

It suddenly became clear to me why I recognized her—I'd seen her picture when going through old family photos. I was never able to ascertain the exact date on the photos but judging by the vintage cars that shared the lens, they must have been taken in the 1930s. She was always with another woman who was equally stunning, and many times they were both with a rather rakish looking man who seemed to possess both money and self confidence, both of which would have come in handy when trying to bag a couple of lookers like those in the pictures.

The other woman who accompanied her this time was not the one who shared those 1930s photographs, though she was equally beautiful in a 1950s-era dress and saddle shoes with white socks.

...This woman, however, was very familiar to me...this woman was my mother. Yes, a much

younger version than what I had grown up with, but no doubt, it was my mother.

The woman I did not know seemed completely indifferent to my presence. There seemed to be arrogance in her stare, much like the look I had seen in the pictures and she gazed through me with an uninterested stare that immediately brought to mind a passage from the play Our Town by Thornton Wilder, in which the stage manager notes:

"You know as well as I do that the dead don't stay interested in us living people for very long. Gradually, gradually, they lose hold on the earth… and the ambitions they had…and the pleasures they had…and the things they suffered…and the people they loved.

They get weaned away from earth…that's the way I put it—weaned away."

That is what I saw in her eyes, a total lack of interest in what was happening. She was here to accompany a friend on a chore, nothing else. But what was it?

My mother had not looked directly at me at this point, her interest was on the dogs. She knelt down petted them and seemed to send them on their way; she called one by name as she praised them. Did I hear it right? Pixie..?

Could it be? My mind raced as I tried to think of the names of all my boyhood dogs, Pixie, Smokey, Brandy…Pixie and what?

That would have to wait. My mother stood up and began to walk my way, the other woman just stood where she had been since they emerged from the door. As my mother approached, I admired her beauty; she was simply stunning. She looked like she did in the photographs from her high school years. I had seen many of them and as I'd looked repeatedly through the years at those old photos, I thought I had a grasp of how attractive she was. I was wrong. The pictures did not do her justice. No wonder my father was so smitten with her as a young man.

She stopped about ten feet away. She would come no closer.

"Is it...?"

"Yes, it's me," she said, before I could even get the words from my mouth.

"Where are you?" I asked.

"A place...not yet for you," she said rather casually.

"Why now? Why me?" I asked.

"It's time to let it go now..." she paused, the words hanging in the air as if they were filled with helium.

"What...?"

"It's time to let it go now, Larry."

"Go to him..." she said.

With that she smiled a sly smile, turned and walked back into the school building with the other woman, never looking back. I watched helplessly as the doors closed and the two shadowy figures began to fade once again into the light.
My eyes flew open, my breathing quickened and

just like that it was over. When I gathered my bearings, I was lying in bed once again with my wife next to me, my heart was racing, and I felt as if I had just had a shot of adrenalin.

As I lay there, I determined that the night must be almost over, but it was still very dark in the room. I looked over to the window in our bedroom and there was no hint of sunrise peaking through the darkness. I looked at the clock. I had only been asleep about three hours—it was 2:45 am.

I spent the next hour trying to figure out what had happened. I came to no solid conclusions. Was it a dream or was it real? It seemed real enough, but most everyone has had dreams that seemed real. No, it was likely random impulses shooting through my brain, the same ones that cause dreams, nightmares, and whatever else goes on in men's tortured souls while they sleep. I may never know for sure.

I thought briefly, with a sense of foreboding about the next day's visit to the hospital in Ellinwood, but I was soon once again crossing the threshold between consciousness and a peaceful sleep...

BLESSING OR CURSE?

Americans today are much more likely to have a planned or natural death than at any time in our history. Why is this? There are several reasons. Many tie back to better government regulations and improved health care. Before we discuss this further let us examine the myriad ways in which we might die an unnatural or unplanned death.
- Vehicle accidents
- Aircraft accidents
- Recreational vehicle accidents (i.e., boats, all-terrain vehicles, motorcycles)
- Work-related accidents
- Sudden heart-related deaths

- Hunting-related accidents.
- Domestic or criminal violence
- Drug-related deaths
- War

What specifically has lowered the number of unplanned deaths in our society? The following are some examples of societal and governmental influences that have resulted in drastically lowering the numbers of sudden or unplanned deaths.

- More government regulations, agencies such as Occupational Health and Safety Administration, Environmental Protection Agency, and the Federal Aviation Administration, to name a few.
- A more paranoid society and business community. Companies and individuals are more aware of safety and liability issues than ever before, due to our litigious society, making the workplace safer and resulting in fewer accidents and deaths.
- Better health care, particularly cardiovascular health, which has prevented many violent and unexpected heart episodes that would otherwise have caused death..
- Groups such as Mothers Against Drunk Drivers (MADD) that have made our roads and children safer from alcohol-related accidents. Additionally, special events such as after-prom parties have made that special night safer for teens as well.
- A more urbanized society in which we live in closer proximity to and have better access to health care than in the more agrarian and rural landscapes of the early twentieth century.
- Military and technological superiority, resulting in fewer battlefield deaths.

As a result, we are much more likely than ever to die a natural death, or more importantly and significantly, a planned death. We are likely to have the time and opportunity to make decisions in relation to how we die, and understand how our death will impact and influence those who have been part of our lives.

WHAT'S THE PLAN?

I would venture to guess that when my uncle developed his thoughts and maybe even a plan on how he would spend his last days, that it did not include me. Yes, he was a close uncle, but he would have naturally and rightfully been more focused on the needs of his wife, children, and grandchildren. I am confident that Junior was glad I was part of his final days, but I don't think it was as important to him as it was to me.

Take my presence out of my Uncle Junior's last week of life and his final days would not have been diminished significantly. But take Uncle Junior's final days out of my life and I would have been impacted dramatically, although I would never have realized it.

What is significant to note is that my uncle had no idea what impact his death was going to have on me and on the remainder of my life. This is why it is so vitally important that we think about and plan those final days. We may not—and probably won't—realize the impact our death can have on those around us. Possibilities include:

- Reconciliation of long disputed family issues
- People learning to hold on to what is important, because time is fleeting
- People finding God, through the pain and challenges of death
- People ultimately coming to terms with their own mortality and our powerlessness in relation to it
- Securing finances at the time of your death through life insurance.

I noted earlier in the book that people fall in love and bond forever at the time of a child's birth. I take that a step further by theorizing that we many times "finish falling in love" with people through the process of their death. The same things we fall in love with in a baby are the same things that bring us closer to a person who is dying. There is a helplessness that both parties feel in the face of death, and bonding occurs as both or all hold on with all possible strength in the face of the onslaught.

In the final analysis, it is not only what is happening with the dying person that's important. Many times what is happening to those people around them, their loved ones, is just as important. And until we truly understand this we cannot truly live a good death.

Hospice organizations are extremely good at guiding families and loved ones through this process, helping them understand that death is not only something that happens to the person who is dying but is a process that everyone close to them goes through as well. It is not easy, it is not painless, and it is not pleasant, but in its own way it is always remarkable and many times life changing. If we do this last thing correctly, then what dies in one person is more than replaced with a new spirit in others, and a closeness to an ultimate destiny and divinity.

THE LIFE ROOM

In dramatic Hollywood fashion, many movies depict the room in which a person departs this earth as a death chamber where it is always dark and stormy. I would like to replace this notion with the image of what I refer to as the "life room." The life room will be a room where death will not be feared or ignored, but where life will be celebrated and acknowledged.

All are welcome, but do not enter with a heavy heart, for this is a time of celebration. The celebration of a life well lived.

This is the sentiment that I plan to have posted at the entrance of my life room as a signal that my impending death is not to be mourned, but my life to be celebrated within these doors and at any services to follow.

This room could be wherever your final days might take place, hopefully in your home. If your final days do not permit, this same room could be set up in the home where people will visit upon your death or maybe even at the funeral home itself. Many variations are possible, but the same types of things would be on display in any circumstance.

- Favorite jokes (written and clean)
- Favorite Music
- Favorite photographs
- A book for visitors to share favorite memories with the family

- Favorite artifacts from the person's life (awards, trophies, correspondence etc.)
- Letters, pre-written by the dying person, for those closest to you to pick up when they come to visit, or they could be delivered after your passing
- Favorite Movies
- School or educational yearbooks
- Educational degrees earned throughout your life
- Your resume and timeline/biography of your life

While these would normally be done in the case of a planned death, there is no reason a life room could not be put together by your family members in the event of a sudden death.

One of the most important things accomplished with a life room is providing people something positive to do when visiting the dying person. It cuts down on the awkwardness that people feel, not knowing what to say to the family or the person who is dying. It takes the focus off death and puts it on the celebration of life.

Part Four

Winter Corridors—The Eulogy

Winter…winter brings us to the last corridors we will walk. The corridors of nursing homes, funeral homes, retirement communities, grandchildren, and our children's first homes.

These corridors will lead to humility, faith, understanding, maturity, and a renewed sense of wonder at the world and finally a deepening of our emotions and faith that can only come with a scarcity of time.

Chapter 1

The Eulogy—Write Your Own

I gently reached down to touch Uncle Junior's hand. He did not wake immediately, so I gently grasped his hand and held it. His eyes began to open, and he looked at me and smiled.

"Hello Larry, How are you?" My Uncle Junior asked

"Fine Uncle Junior," I said rather unsteadily, although I probably sounded more confident than I felt.

I took immediate notice that it was going to be difficult for him to talk, so I asked him if it would be alright for me to stay and watch some golf with him (that is what was on television when I walked in). I knew this would help curb the awkwardness I felt, and take the pressure off him to feel he had to converse.

He said that would be wonderful and that he would enjoy the company.

As I sat in the guest chair pretending to care what was going on half a country away in Augusta, Georgia, and even, on occasion, making rather enthusiastic comments about a particular shot or two, I couldn't help but wonder how I could put into words what this man had meant to my life at that stage. I didn't realize that the best, most dramatic event was yet to come.

When an important person dies, there is no shortage of people who will gladly sing that persons praises, and if they are important enough, many flowery speeches are made to recognize their life and accomplishments. There would be none of this for my Uncle Junior. I didn't believe he would have felt comfortable with that attention and rarely are those kind of speeches made for an average person.

I couldn't help but reflect on a song by Emerson Lake and Palmer (yes, I liked a little rock and roll in my day) called "Fanfare for the Common Man." It was a very dramatic song that one might expect to be written for a head of state or someone of that stature, but was instead a wonderful ballad that paid tribute to all the common people—those who will never see their faces grace the cover of a magazine, will probably never have their "fifteen minutes of fame," and most likely will never be properly thanked for all the good they do in their lifetime. However, they are the very people who do most of the working, living, and dying in our society. Junior should have had someone do an eloquent tribute to his life and it saddened me that at that time in my life, I did not have the communication skills to pay tribute in a manner that he deserved.

The sound of light snoring had brought me back to the room, back to the reality of my situation. I might not be able to pay a formal tribute to my uncle at his funeral, but I could at least in my own awkward way pay him the respect he deserved personally. After all, this could well be my last time to say such words. The cancer was quickly winning the battle…it wouldn't be long now.

When I got up to leave, Junior sensed my motion and his eyes fluttered open briefly.

"Junior," I said.

His eyed fluttered and then opened. Finally his gaze became fixed and focused on my face.

"I have to go now," I continued, "but before I do I wanted to let you know how impressed I am with the way you have lived your life, and especially with the grace and courage you have shown these final weeks."

At that point he squeezed my hands and unceremoniously recited the seventeen words that would change my life forever...

A few years ago I went to the funeral of a wealthy, successful businessman in Great Bend. The funeral was fairly uneventful until the moment an attorney, representing the deceased businessman, got up and delivered his eulogy. What made this especially unique is that the eulogy was crafted entirely by the departed before his death. It was remarkable. He talked about some key events in his life, people who had been important to him, and most importantly he told his family how much he loved them and how proud he was of each of them. What a wonderful last gift to give to those you love, to hear from you at your funeral just how much you loved each of them.

Each person is unique, so it would be impossible for me to instruct each of you how to craft your own eulogy. However, I can show you how I would envision mine to read. If I were to die tomorrow, this is how my eulogy would read. And just as one would update a will, this too would change over time.

———

Anyone who truly knew me should have known I would find a way to get the last word, even at my own funeral. As I move into the next stage of my journey, I am filled with a sense of awe and wonder, happiness and yes…sorrow.

Awe and wonder—in respect to what lies ahead, the realization that I am about to get all the answers to all the questions. As a student of life, this excites and inspires me in ways that I cannot describe. Happiness—in that I am about to be rejoined with those I love who have passed before me. The sorrow, of course, comes from the realization that I am leaving behind treasured family and friends as well as many things and ways of living that I hold dear.

My death can be paralleled to the emotions I experienced when my family moved from Great Bend to Salina. While I was excited at the challenges that lay ahead, and the new opportunities that would surely present themselves, simultaneously I knew I was going to miss my previous surroundings, my family, friends, and neighbors immeasurably. I always prided myself, after our move to Salina, that I did not forget where I came from. I always kept a foothold in my hometown because I cared for it deeply. In that same respect I will keep a spiritual foothold in my previous life by keeping a watch on those I love, while awaiting the day that we can be reunited.

Throughout my life I have been a son, father, brother, husband, student, teacher, athlete, author, musician, businessman, and community leader. While I am obviously proud of each of those roles, my family has always been my rock, my stability, and the center of my universe.

My wife Julie, my college sweetheart, life partner, and woman who has provided me joy that cannot be described. My children Hillary and Brantley who have provided me such pride and joy as well as a bond both special and inseparable. They truly brought to me a depth of emotion I never thought I could attain; they helped teach me to love. My parents Wally, Barbara, and Betty who each in their own way taught me all of life's lessons. My brothers and sisters and their spouses—Ron and Kathy, Linda and Brad, Beverly and Clyde, and Donna and Mike—who taught me that you can count on people no matter what. My nieces and nephews—Jesse, David, Audrey, Darren, Kristy, and Jeffrey—who taught me how to stay young and full of life. I thank you all, my family, for teaching me and showing me every day what unconditional love is all about.

If you will permit me a final act of this earth, I will fulfill one last time a role I hold dear, that of teacher. Life is at its best a joy and at its worst a challenge. Death at its best is a challenge. However, today I want to ask each of you to allow me to teach one more lesson by my passing. The lesson…death is as much a part of living as life itself.

When you experience a sudden death or are involved in the process of a person's passing, I challenge you to look around and pay attention to all the incredible things that happen surrounding that event. Try to look through the pain and into the light. With each death, wondrous things take place: families gather and some find long overdue reconciliations, people learn to treasure what they have because it is fleeting, and finally we learn to love a little deeper.

When a baby is born, we fall in love for life. There is no separating that bond. When someone we care deeply about dies, we many times finish the process of falling in love. We find a depth to our emotions that is born out of a scarcity of time. When we no longer have the luxury of unlimited time, we say things long overdue, we do things that can no longer wait, and we experience feelings that could not be explored or expressed in our normal lives. As time grows short it is no longer possible to take anything for granted. Time becomes more precious, emotions are intensified, and we find an even deeper bond than we thought possible.

I believe this is what defines this journey known as life. I believe this is why good people die, some much too early. It is God's way of teaching us to love ultimately and without reservation, a love that can only be fully experienced and learned through the process and event of death.

In closing, to those of you who may have caused me harm, all is forgiven. To those of you that I may have caused harm, please accept this, my final apology. To those of you who have made my life such a joy, I say thank you, and God bless…

Epilogue

At that point he squeezed my hands and unceremoniously recited the seventeen words that would change my life forever...

"I've taught my kids how to live, now it is time to teach them how to die..."

As I walked out of my uncle's room and back down the hall, a hall that now seemed much shorter than it did earlier, my steps much lighter, I could not get those words out of my head.

"...now it is time to teach them how to die..." Junior had said the words rather casually, almost dismissively.

They seemed important at the time, even then some of the most profound words I had ever heard; in fact, their significance was not lost on me. However, there was no way I could have known just what those seventeen words would mean to my life.

How those seventeen words would bridge a gap of seventeen years and bring to a culmination much of the uncertainty that had been with me since my mother's death, allowing me to move on, to live my life to the fullest and learn.

Learn the lessons that death can teach us about life.

As I draw this book to its conclusion, I remain mindful of the fact that I am in my own way expanding on my uncle's final life's work. Attempting to teach people by challenging their perspective on what constitutes both a good life and a good death.

As I have written this book, I have done so with a great deal of humility. This humility comes in three forms. First, I have no right to cast judgment on peoples' belief systems or force mine onto them. I have attempted to put together a book that would have something in it for people of most religious faiths. This was a broad goal, but it was in fact a sincere goal. I will leave the judging to others; there are plenty who are much more qualified than I, and more than eager to do so.

Second, I would not give the reader any delusions about this being a program to live by. It is not. It is not a one-size-fits-all, "do this for thirty days and your life will be improved beyond recognition" book. It is not even a book in which you have to accept all of what I have to say. I have no doubt that some of what I say will be controversial. I have tried to compartmentalize ideas and concepts in such a way that you can take what makes sense and throw the rest to the side (feel free to metaphorically burn them if you like).

My goal has been to provide a viewpoint that could at least be considered. Some of the topics I discuss are not complete in my own mind—I am still formulating my opinions and am unclear how I will feel regarding a few of these subjects ten years from now.

Certain parts or concepts laid out in this book may be irrelevant to you now, but may prove valuable to you later in life. The letter I referred to in the forward of the book, from a former student, is an example of someone who did not see the relevance of this story initially, but as her life circumstances changed, certain things came into focus that had not been present earlier.

I am not selling my ideas or trying to convince the reader about truth. I only hope that if you find a couple or more ideas or concepts that ring true, that will make this book worth the time you have spent reading it.

The final area in which I feel humbled is, finally, an admitted lack of experience in the matters I write about. I have been intimately involved in two deaths, and have been a distant participant in some others. I readily admit that I am relatively naïve in comparison to many other people but I believe I was able to unearth answers that can help people in need deal with such issues. While it was tempting for me to wait to write this book—until I had more life and death experience—it didn't feel right for me to delay any longer. I felt it could provide answers and comfort for many, most importantly those closest to me, my family and friends. Writing this book now was a risk I had to take.

The good Lord willing, I fully intend to update this work twenty years from now. At that time I will unfortunately have had more experience with death and will also have had another twenty years of experiences of other kinds. It will be intriguing to see how well my perceptions, practices, and theories have stood the test of time—in the world and in my life.

THE FAMILY

I am glad and very proud to report that this book has a happy ending in one respect. Both the Schartz and the Straub families have produced healthy, happy, well-adjusted people and citizens. Both families have had our share of trials, but none that were insurmountable. Overall, life has been good for both the Straub and the Schartz families and hopefully will remain so well into the future.

IN CLOSING

Throughout the writing of this book, I embarked on a road of self-discovery. Along the way I have formulated many concepts that will help me find closure in my life on several fronts. First, I came to terms with the death of my mother. Second, I found possible answers to why bad things happen to good people. And finally, I began to see how we can learn from all the life events thrown our way, both the good and the bad.

I want to assure all who read this book that throughout this project my heart and soul have been aligned, and I believe my intentions have been good. My ultimate goal has been to help people find a path through some of the most difficult times any of us will ever experience, the death of a loved one. May God, your own determination, and possibly some of what you have learned from this book help you find your own path through the darkness and into the light.

> *As I made the journey back to Great Bend from Ellinwood the last night Junior was to be on this earth, I pulled over at my traditional location, two miles west of town, same dirt road, same spot.*
>
> *This time no tears would come. I was spent, my tear ducts finally exhausted.*
>
> *No tears…not this time.*
>
> *However as I sat there once again, I reflected on all that had just happened and the effect it would inevitably have on my life. The realization of what it would mean would have to wait. And it would finally reveal itself in the form of a little book…this book.*

Those seventeen words spoken seventeen years after my mother's death would finally be solidified in my consciousness seventeen years later with the publishing of this book… Autumn Corridors.

> *The telephone ringing cut through the darkness like a slashing knife and into my consciousness just as ferociously. I fumbled around, trying to get my bearings and my focus. Finally I was able to get a fix on the clock—2:45 am. (At the time, I didn't register the irony of that being the exact time the dream involving my mother ended just a night earlier, surely coincidental.)*
>
> *About this time my wife nudged me in the ribs. In the division of labor that naturally occurs in any marriage, I had drawn the duty of answering early morning phone calls. "Phone!" she called out groggily.*

Only two kinds of calls are made at this time of the morning. Drunken adolescents finally getting up the artificial courage to call an old girlfriend and attempt a reconciliation...and the other kind.

It didn't take much imagination or prophetic ability to figure out what this one was about.

"Larry this is Uncle Allen (Junior's younger bother). Junior just passed away, about fifteen minutes ago. He was in no pain and it was very peaceful."

"Thanks, Al, and God Bless."

As I hung up the phone, I felt a sense of peace and happiness. Junior's battle was over and his life's journey successfully completed...

I also felt in that same moment that mine was just beginning anew.

Yes we will walk them all, the intriguing and treacherous corridors of life. And if we are lucky, we will not walk alone.

We will walk with parents, children, grandchildren, neighbors, friends, and teachers.

And hopefully and through it all, we will walk with the Prince of Peace,

the Great 'I Am.'